No Turning Back

SURVIVING THE LINEHAN FAMILY TRAGEDY

IDA LINEHAN YOUNG

We gratefully acknowledge the financial support of the Canada Council for the Arts, the Government of Canada through the Canada Book Fund (CBF), and the Government of Newfoundland and Labrador through the Department of Tourism, Culture and Recreation for our publishing program.

Printed on acid-free paper
Cover design & layout by Todd Manning

Published by
CREATIVE PUBLISHERS
an imprint of CREATIVE BOOK PUBLISHING
a Transcontinental Inc. associated company
P.O. Box 8660, Stn. A
St. John's, Newfoundland and Labrador A1B 3T7

Printed in Canada

Second printing, September, 2014

Library and Archives Canada Cataloguing in Publication

Linehan Young, Ida, 1964-, author
No turning back : surviving the Linehan family tragedy / Ida Linehan Young.

ISBN 978-1-77103-056-4 (pbk.)

1. Linehan Young, Ida, 1964-. 2. Linehan Young, Ida, 1964- --Homes and haunts. 3. Burns and scalds--Patients--Newfoundland and Labrador--North Harbour (Saint Mary's Bay)--Biography. 4. Fires--Casualties--Newfoundland and Labrador--North Harbour (Saint Mary's Bay). 5. Fires--Newfoundland and Labrador--North Harbour (Saint Mary's Bay). 6. Home accidents--Newfoundland and Labrador--North Harbour (Saint Mary's Bay). 7. Bereavement--Psychological aspects. 8. North Harbour (Saint Mary's Bay, N.L.)--Biography. I. Title.

FC2199.N673Z49 2014   363.3709718   C2014-904690-1

No Turning Back

SURVIVING THE LINEHAN FAMILY TRAGEDY

IDA LINEHAN YOUNG

CREATIVE PUBLISHERS

St. John's, Newfoundland and Labrador
2014

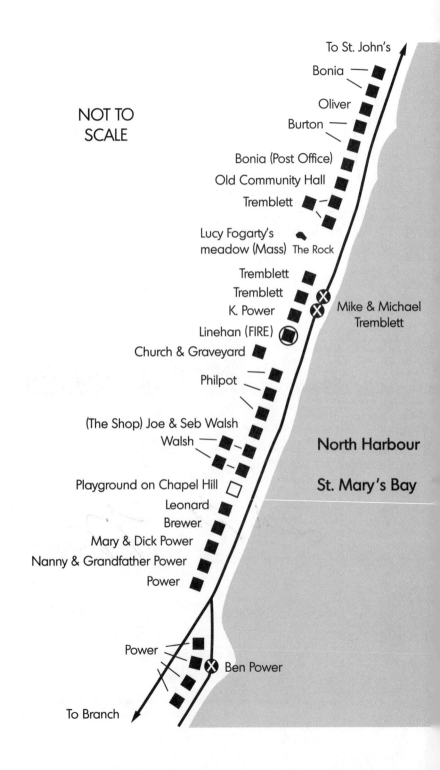

To St. John's

Bonia

Oliver

Burton

Bonia (Post Office)

Old Community Hall

Tremblett

NOT TO
SCALE

Lucy Fogarty's
meadow (Mass)   The Rock

Tremblett

Tremblett

K. Power

Linehan (FIRE)

Church & Graveyard

Mike & Michael
Tremblett

Philpot

(The Shop) Joe & Seb Walsh

Walsh

North Harbour

St. Mary's Bay

Playground on Chapel Hill

Leonard

Brewer

Mary & Dick Power

Nanny & Grandfather Power

Power

Power

Ben Power

To Branch

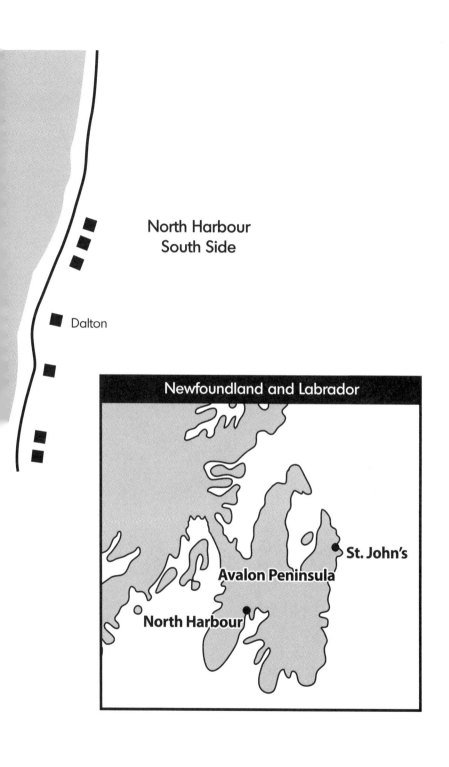

North Harbour
South Side

Dalton

Newfoundland and Labrador

St. John's

Avalon Peninsula

North Harbour

Linehan Property

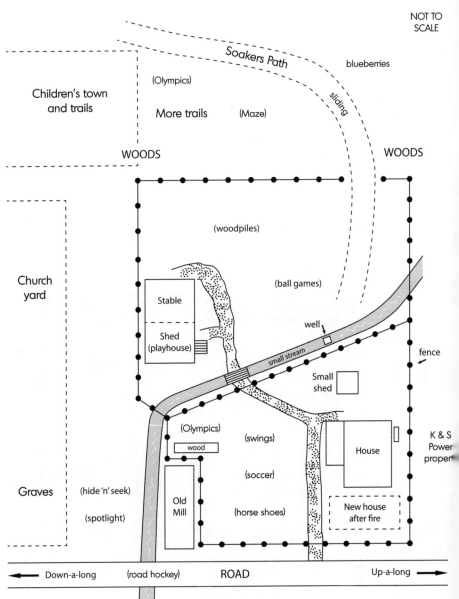

To all my Linehan siblings both living and deceased, I dedicate this book.

Francis, Richard, Sharon, Harold and Barry your short lives had a great impact that has stayed with many of us including family, friends, co-workers and classmates all our lives. I hope this book will give those who never knew you a peek at why we were all so affected by your loss.

Mary, as a big sister you can overcome any challenges in this life. I love you and your son Scott.

Eddy, you are always kind and we both have had a special connection from forever. I love you and Irena, Anna and Patrick.

Neil, your quiet perspective on this whole tragic series of life-changing events is powerful. I love you and Trudy, Shayne and Kirsten and their families.

Larry, you have had more to deal with in your lifetime than anyone will ever know, I admire your strength. I love you and Caroline.

To my parents Eddy and Catherine (Power) Linehan, I dedicate this book.

No words can be written that will convey the loss you suffered and how you stood strong and protected us over the years. I love you Mom and I love you Dad in heaven.

To my husband, Thomas Young, I dedicate this book.

Thomas we have not had an easy life but I wouldn't want to go through it with anyone else, I love you. Thank you for your love, encouragement and support.

To my children, I dedicate this book.

Sharon, I have loved you the longest and I love the beautiful woman you have become. You can accomplish anything and have a special guardian angel.

Stacey, I love your kind heart. Trust that heart, you are awesome – you will show the world what I know when you get "discovered".

Shawna, I love the baby who has blossomed into a beautiful funny young woman. You will make an amazing, confident mother.

Lastly, I dedicate this book to the wonderful people of North Harbour.

If every community had the "North Harbour Gene" we would all be better off. Thanks for being my True North and my haven in hard times.

Ida

Preface

In the early morning hours of June 19th, 1980 a tragedy unfolded in the tiny community of North Harbour, St. Mary's Bay. It haunts people to this day. Over thirty years later it is very difficult to get people to talk about what happened those many years before.

Early that morning, Mike Tremblett and his son Michael were getting ready to go fishing and were in the beach a few hundred feet from the Linehan house. Mike looked up and saw smoke in the sky over the hill and told his son that he believed "Eddy's house was afire."

Mike went to the house while Michael alerted the older couple who were the nearest neighbours then got his own wife and family up before going to help his father.

At the other end of the Harbour, Ben Power was also getting ready to go fishing and, seeing the smoke, he used binoculars to approximate the location of the Linehan house. He got his wife Dorothy out of bed and told her to start calling people as he jumped in his truck and headed up through the Harbour with his horn blaring to alert the neighbours that something was wrong.

Within the next few minutes, as neighbours began to arrive, the house was destroyed by fire.

For the people who read about this tragedy in 1980 that may have been the end of it, a passing thought and perhaps a prayer for those poor people and what they must be suffering.

For the people who lived through it, and the people who lived with it, it was only the beginning.

For me it was a long and painful journey. If you venture onward I will take you from the raging inferno, through my time in the hospital and a healing process culminating many years later in my own forgiveness of myself for living.

This book is written from the eyes and from the emotions of one who lived it – me! It is a genuine account in great detail of things I know, things I learned as I went, and things that I didn't know until the very recent past as I put together the story of my family, the Linehans of North Harbour.

Linehan Family Tree

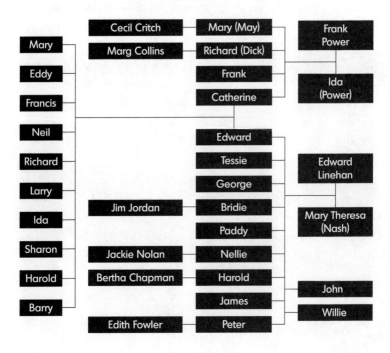

Linehan Home Floorplans

1ST FLOOR

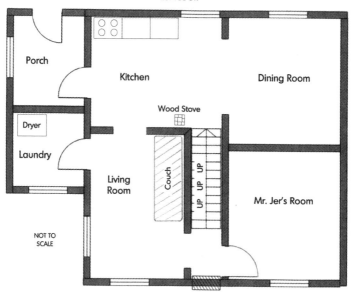

2ND FLOOR

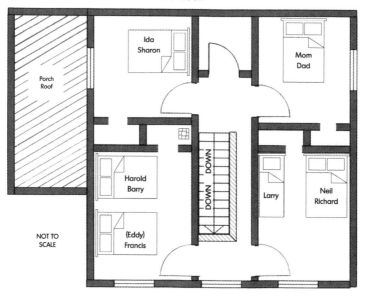

June 19, 1980

I awoke with a sense that something was wrong. My mind didn't seem like it was working; I tried to shake off the sleep and focus on what had forced me from my slumber. My brain was foggy, my eyes were stinging and there was a strange smell in the air.

Then I heard it, my mother shouting out over and over, what sounded like, for everyone to get up. I turned my head toward the sound and rose up on my elbow but I still couldn't focus. I wasn't quite sure what she was saying or why she would be up. My mother's bare feet, calves and the bottom of her light blue cotton night dress were visible at the top of the stairway just outside our open bedroom door but there was something wrong. The rest of her body was hidden in an unusual haze. I looked toward the window and it was daylight however the window appeared eerily strange like there were dark clouds floating on the inside in our room.

I turned my head and followed my mother's voice again as she kept shouting, "Everyone get up and come to me, the house is on fire!" She was coughing and repeating that over the noise that I could now hear – a crackling and roaring of some kind began to pound in my ears. There was a strange heat in the room, beyond any I had ever felt before.

Something was terribly wrong, the house was on fire!

I rolled off my elbow and sat straight up in bed, my head groggy as I gulped in air, only then realizing it was hard to breathe. The smell of black tar and smoke drenched my senses and I knew I had to get up but I was unable to get myself oriented.

A memory popped into my head: our family had talked about our escape route in the event of a fire and it had been plotted to this bedroom, our bedroom. We were to get out on the roof of the porch that was attached to our two-storey house beneath my bedroom window and climb to safety from there as it was the lowest point on the house from the upstairs rooms.

I realized that I had to get to the window. My sister Sharon was in the bed with me and I shook her awake and told her there was trouble, we had to get out. She didn't seem to be aware of her surroundings so I scrambled out of the bed and came around to the other side. I grabbed her, pulling at her arms and shoulders until I finally managed to stand her by the bedside. She stayed erect although she did not move and did not make a sound. I took her hand and placed it around the foot of the bed frame that rose up like a small iron pillar from the floor. My protective instinct kicked in and I told her to stay there until I broke the window and that I would come back for her. She did not move or seem to comprehend what was happening and stood there as if she were a statue.

At fourteen years old Sharon was eighteen months my junior and was my best friend along with being my sister. Although we quarrelled on occasion, I always looked out for her and we shared everything, including a room and a bed. We played together, went mostly everywhere together and it had been that way for as long as I could remember.

As I looked towards the hall I noticed that my mom was gone and I could see the smoke getting thicker and barreling up the stairs. *Get to the porch* was my plan, *get to the porch and get us both out.*

6

I felt my way to the window with my hands outstretched and looked out through the ever-thickening smoke; it still seemed so unreal at this point.

There was a makeshift book case beneath the window made from Carnation Milk cardboard boxes coated with a red rose-patterned wallpaper and which had cardboard shelves taped inside. Proudly displayed on this handmade bookshelf were several trophies from cross-country running and academics that both Sharon and I had received over the last couple of years from our high school, Our Lady of Mount Carmel.

It was difficult to see, my eyes were burning and it was getting harder to breathe. As I tried to concentrate on my movements the noise around me was getting louder, the smoke was getting thicker and the combination seemed to be urging me to hurry. However, I was groggy and every movement seemed as if I was in slow motion.

The bottom window sash slid upwards but I knew that it only went a few inches because it had been painted so often and usually warped in damp weather or after the Spring of the year. I tried to pull it upward but it would not open wide enough to allow us to get out so I pushed it shut again.

I grabbed the tallest trophy from the bookcase and swung it at the glass. In mid-motion I thought about how Mom would be so mad at me for breaking the window even though I knew that I would be forgiven for this.

When the trophy struck the glass, it didn't explode outward as I had anticipated but sort of fell downward on the windowsill inside and outside with a strange cracking noise like two knives rubbing together. We had broken many windows while out playing games in the yard and this was not what I had heard before.

The sound of tinkling glass on glass as pieces slid over each other when gravity took over broke through the growing noise from inside the house. I used the trophy to hit at some of the sharp edges of the glass inside the lower windowpane to clear it; putty and glass fell inside and out. I threw the trophy on the floor in the corner to my right and pushed the other trophies in the same direction with one swing of my arm, hearing the crash as they fell to the floor. Then I stuck my head outside while leaning over the box-bookcase.

I was grateful that Dad had removed the storm windows because that would have added an extra layer of glass and a further complication.

I gasped as the clean air filled my lungs and I began to understand just how bad the smoke and heat was inside. I planted my two hands on the windowsill not worrying about the shards of glass, craning my neck upwards as I drank in the air. I could feel the heat of the black smoke pushing on my back as it tried to escape above and around me. I heard a hollow boom from inside the house as air searched for and found flame.

I looked around trying to assess the situation outside and noticed that the entire eave of the porch beneath my window had flames flickering just about everywhere and the black smoke was piling out incessantly as if a dark beast had just been released.

The black-tarred felt coating on the roof of the porch was not fully engulfed but the edges were catching around the eaves and curling upward. I could reach the roof once I kicked away the cardboard bookcase which I promptly did with my bare foot.

I leaned ahead and placed the palms of my hands on the tarred roof. It felt very hot and sticky to the touch and I knew that this was not going to be the way out. I believed the whole roof must have been on fire underneath. I was afraid that if we got out on the roof it would collapse into the fire and we would be doomed.

I bent lower to get myself back in the room so that I wouldn't hit the top of the wooden window sash. When my head came up inside the bedroom, reflexes forced me back out the window gulping for more fresh air.

My mind changed gears at this point. I started to repeat over and over in my head as if in a chant, *you can't stay here, you can't stay here …* to try and force my body to obey. As I pulled back in through the window for the second time I struggled to remain there and I knew I had to get both myself and Sharon out of here as soon as possible.

As I turned to go back to the bed to get Sharon, I could barely make out a figure coming towards me in the black smoke-filled room against the faint orange backdrop now glowing near the floor in the hall.

At first I thought it was Sharon but then Larry, my older brother, came running at the window without seeing me. I could make out the frightened look on his face and the urgency in his gait as he neared. As I stepped aside to avoid collision he pushed his head and upper torso out the window and was trying to get his leg up to climb out on the roof. When I realized he was attempting to get out, I grabbed on to his bare back and dug in my fingers to tug him backward into the room. My fingertips slid across the blackened skin on his back before finally taking hold.

Larry felt me pulling on him and I cried out over the noise of the rushing air and crackling sounds that the roof was on fire and wasn't safe. Since he wasn't fully in the room, he looked out again, paused and came back inside. I shouted to go back and try to get out some other way. He turned and was gone back into the still deepening blackness and out into the hall.

My mind was beginning to get fuzzy again. I was trying not to gasp for air and was taking deep breaths in the smoke. Down by my feet seemed to be less black and so was the closet, which was directly behind me. I backed up into the closet and crouched down as far as I could and took some more breaths. The air didn't seem to be pushing towards the opening in the window in here like it was in the bedroom so it was easier to breathe although still smoky.

Almost instinctively my body ached to curl up in a fetal position and stay there but I forced myself to keep repeating in my mind, *you can't stay here, you can't stay here* ... and I knew that in fact, I couldn't stay there. I thought of Sharon somewhere close in the blackness and probably scared. I could see her bare feet on the floor close by near the bed where I had left her to wait for me. I had to get out and I had to get her out.

I forced myself to move swiftly, struggling against an instinct that was telling me to stay. I stood up, stretched my arms out in front of me and felt my way the few steps towards the bed. The canvas-covered floorboards were hot under my feet and I continued to struggle for breath but I refused to give up. I had to get us out.

The room wasn't very big; it had a double bed, a tall dresser, and the Carnation Milk box-bookcase that I was sure was now in pieces in the corner to the right of the window. I slept on the inside of the bed towards the wall and there was room for me to get in and out. The head of the bed was on the wall next to the door and Sharon slept on that side. The door to the hall swung inwards and the dresser was beside the door leaving room to access the tiny closet. When Mary was home from St. John's on the weekends she shared the room with us, we being the only three girls in the family of ten siblings.

Sharon was in the same place I had left her and she was still very quiet. I could feel her and make out her shape in the darkness as I grabbed one hand and tried to pull her along with me out of the room.

She resisted a little at first so I pried her fingers on the other hand from the bedrail and she didn't try to hold her ground; she came with me as if she were a small child being led along. She was very slow but she had not had any fresh air as I did when I stuck my head out the window. We couldn't go back that way now for air because flames were starting to lick at the window frame from the outside as fire climbed that side of the house. It was not the way out!

As I exited the bedroom I could make out the stairwell – the flames were like great orange octopus arms coming around the archway from the living room at the bottom, pushing up around the stairs. The flames seemed alive like they were coming for me. I knew there was no going down even though there was an exterior door right at the bottom of the stairs in my line of vision. That door was never used, nor was the wooden storm door outside it ever opened; it had been nailed shut since the house was built. Regardless, flames were blocking the whole exit and pushing up the stairs. We had to get out from the second floor.

My parents' door across the hall from our bedroom was almost closed. This was normal because the door didn't hang straight and defaulted to slightly ajar. Rational thought eluded me and I didn't try to go in there as we would never go in Mom and Dad's room without permission even though she had been shouting for us to come to her only a few moments before.

Without thinking and almost by habit, I turned to go across by the side of the stairs along the top railing. I had Sharon by the hand but she was slowing down and seemed harder to drag along; however she was still trying. She still never made a sound.

The space got even darker and it was harder than ever to breathe. The extreme heat felt as if the place was ready to implode.

It was amazing how quickly the fire was spreading. There had been no sign of flames when I got out of bed only a minute before. Now they seemed to reach out of the blackness and grab for us. I could see the orange, red and hot white glow through the thick black smoke and felt the stinging on my right arm and upper torso. I pulled back but kept hold of the railing to feel where I was going and had Sharon tucked in behind me with my other hand in hers. I was squeezing her hand hard but hers was limp in mine.

About halfway across the hall, still feeling my way along the stair rail, somebody slammed into me going the other way. He materialized so fast and every breath was now hot black smoke and fire distracting me from what was happening. My lungs were screaming for oxygen, my eyes were burning, and my body wasn't responding the way I wanted it to. The person I banged into had to be one of my brothers and he was also holding the rail, knocking me off. I was sure he had not seen me because I did not see him and I fell back on the wall in the hall but stayed on my feet. I reached out to grab him in the darkness when my hand let go of the rail, but he was gone.

Then, I realized, so was Sharon – she was gone. I lost her somewhere close when I fell back off the rail but I felt around on the bottom of the wall behind me and couldn't find her. I was getting disoriented but I could see, although in a haze, the floor around my feet and she wasn't there. I bent down to feel around some more but the fire was coming through the railing and stinging my face. She just wasn't there. Going back was not an option now as there was no way out back there and I didn't know where she had gone. I had no idea which of my brothers had passed me going the other way and thought maybe she had gone with him.

I stood there for what must have been seconds debating what to do and trying to find her but it seemed much longer. I felt the flames brushing on my shoulder and arm and I pulled back again. I stood up and grabbed hold of the railing as my lifeline and continued in the direction I was headed before I lost Sharon.

For some reason, my shoulder reminded me of what a piece of plastic would feel like, if it could think and feel, when it was burning on a log in the stove – all shrivelling up. The flames were shrivelling my flesh. It was getting darker around me, the noises louder and I knew that I wouldn't last much longer if I didn't get out soon.

I started to chant in my mind again and maybe even out loud – this time it was, *if you panic you will die, if you panic you will die* …

I made myself repeat this over and over and I concentrated on it because the urge to blindly run was almost overwhelming and would surely be the end of me.

I felt the baluster at the far corner of the stairs, and instead of going left, seemingly away from the chaos, into Richard, Neil, and Larry's room, I went to the right, continuing to hold on to the stair railing. There was no explanation for my choice nor was it even a choice – just an action. By now the flames were full force coming up around the floor that I was standing on and were throwing whips of flames against me. The angry beast was here!

The ceiling above my head was on fire. I held back as far as I could but kept my arm stretched out to the railing, *if you panic you will die, if you panic you will die* ... There was a window beside me at the end of the hall with a trunk in front of it but I knew the trunk was heavy and couldn't be moved and that the window hadn't been opened in years. There was too much fire and complications here to give that possibility more than a passing thought. The plastic curtains that hung on the window had long since been melted and daylight was trying to break through the layer of darkness to my left into the bright fire light on my right.

I made it to the open doorway and went inside while letting go of the rail on the stairs. I thought Francis or Eddy might be in here to help as it was their room along with my two younger brothers, Harold and Barry. There was no movement and I shouted out over the roar that was even louder from below. By now my feet were getting very hot and I looked around the room to see what I could do.

My eyes went to their closet where the chimney came up from below and I could see flames etched on the sides and top of that doorframe through the dark smoke. There was no escape route there, but it seemed like an option, remembering how being in my own closet had felt safer. I shook my head and saner thoughts came back.

I turned my attention to the door I had just come in through and by now I could see the flames barrelling in from underneath the floor and up towards the ceiling, which was also on fire. It reminded me of a curve on a huge wave I had seen on the opening credits of the TV show *Hawaii Five-O*, however it was fire, not water, and more menacing. *If you panic you will die, if you panic you will die* ...

There was nothing in front of the window in this room so I moved towards it, only a few steps. Since there was nothing here to hit the pane of glass with, I made a fist and punched it out with my right hand. Fear of being cut was not as strong as the alternative, which was imminent.

The glass again had a weird feel and sound as it was breaking. The hole wasn't big so I made a few more punches at it and my body, seeming to have will of its own and a will to survive, didn't protest at the sharp glass.

I couldn't breathe and in a rush I stuck my head out the jagged hole to get some air, to see what was going on outside on the ground, and to hopefully make my escape. As I pushed my head through the hole in the pane of glass I was immediately hit with flames coming out from the living room window on the first floor. The flames seemed to fill my lungs and my eyes blinked closed.

Reflexes pulled me back and as I was coming through the window I could feel the remaining glass on the top of the window pane rip a line down through my lower back. I was hurting and knew I didn't have much time and this was not the way out. *If you panic you will die, if you panic you will die* ...

I had glimpsed a flurry of activity at the lower window to the left of me and directly under the room across the hall. It was only a flash of an image before my eyes blinked shut but people were out there trying to help.

I looked back at the door I had just come in through and knew this was it – I had to go back. There was fire all around outside the door because I could see the orange and red flames growing and less of the black smoke. Pieces of fire seemed to start from nothing and were dropping everywhere, igniting what they touched and small fires were breaking out around me on the floor and on the beds in the room. Breathing now seemed impossible and I didn't have much strength left in my legs. The roar of the fire was so strong in my ears that I couldn't hear much except the louder crackling, burning wood. My body wanted to give up and lie down but I forced it to move. This was bad. *If you panic you will die, if you panic you will die ...*

I knew I had nothing to lose – it was just as well to die trying as it was to give up. I realized I had to use whatever strength I had in my legs and body to push myself outside the door, across the hall, and into the other room. *If you panic you will die, if you panic you will die ...* raced much faster through my head but I refused to let myself lose control and concentrated on repeating the words. If force of will could move my limbs, I was going.

I paused to see if there would be an ebb in the flames as they rushed over the landing on the top of the stairs. I couldn't see much from this viewpoint through the doorway, but it was enough to know that I might be able to calculate a good time to push forward. But I hesitated for only a moment as I realized it was getting worse and every second was precious.

My breathing was laboured; I was only getting thick black smoke and hot air in my throat and lungs. I was competing with the fire for the little oxygen that was in the house and the fire was quickly winning. This was it, I had to go back the way I came in – through the flames coming up around the stairs.

The flames behind me, which I had given access through the broken window, seemed to be telling me to hurry as they devoured the wall over the window and consumed the ceiling. Now I was surrounded.

I pushed forward. It was probably only eight steps from where I was standing to get to the other room across the top of the stairs.

The flames were a wall coming towards me, in the room, on the ceiling above my head, gorging on everything they touched. The white oil paint on the door frame was bubbling and igniting all at once. *If you panic you will die, if you panic you will die ...*

If I hurried I could make it. Hopefully the floor in the hallway was still strong enough to hold beneath my ninety-pound weight. Because of the trunk I had to keep over towards the worst of the fire but there was no choice and moments were precious.

One step, two steps, I was in the hall and closed my eyes, three, four, five, six, seven ... I gauged I had passed through the worst of the flames because of the slight decrease in the heat in those last few seconds. I was at the open door in the room on the other side of the landing when I peeked from under my eyelids. The smell of burned flesh mixed with the smell of the thick black smoke and I had the sudden urge to vomit.

Several things were going through my head at this time: I was afraid of the distance between the window and the rocky ground so I didn't know if I would jump, or if there was somebody below to help, or if my brothers were in the room and could help me get out; so many things.

When I opened my eyes I realized there was nobody in the room and I was on my own. Little fires were starting to ignite in here now as well. The heat and flames were behind me and coming fast. *If you panic you will die, if you panic you will die ...* The window was to my right and was open or broken out because I could see the smoke rushing out around the top pane of glass – somebody had gone before me. As I took step eight further into the room my oxygen and my time had run out. I started to fall forward, and then there was black.

I don't know how much time passed but I could see myself on the ground and wondered how I had gotten there. There was a strange glow around me that I couldn't explain, but for some reason I was aware I was looking at "me."

Was I dead? Was I alive? I couldn't tell. It was like there was two of me and I began moving away from my body – I wasn't afraid as I was trying to absorb what was happening. A bright fog was forming around me and seemed to be swallowing me up as I moved further away from my body on the ground.

I could see people below but they were getting smaller and smaller and couldn't see me leaving. I thought about shouting but I felt at peace and did not want to let them know I was there or make a sound.

I saw the house as if a camera was shooting a movie and I was hovering above looking through the lens. The smoke and flames were pushing out through every window and around the eaves of the porch and the house. People were running everywhere and there I was, lying on the ground where I must have landed after the fall.

My body on the ground seemed like it was glowing as I floated away in the bright fog. Was this a dream, had this been a dream like the night before? I could barely hear something and concentrated to make it out. The sound was getting fainter and fainter as I moved further and further away. I felt very strange and unreal – relaxed, quiet, and unhurt; it must have been a dream. I tried to shift my focus to whoever was shouting, but it wasn't easy.

"She's dead, she's dead!" I heard my mother yelling, and suddenly, as if I was suctioned in, I was back in my body, no longer watching the scene from above. I opened my eyes.

People were shouting orders or just shouting because there was too much chaos to make out what anyone was actually saying or who they were. The noise coming from inside the house had followed me and so had the heat.

Confusion surrounded me and I was on the rocks looking up at my mother, who had just run around the corner of the house as I landed at her feet. She told me later that it was like having a rubber sack full of water thrown down – the thud was sickening as I landed on my back on the rocky ground beneath the window. She thought I was dead.

There was a crowd near my head, oblivious to me lying there. They had just gotten our boarder, Mr. Jer (Jeremiah Bonia), out of his room, which was directly below the one I had just come out from on the second floor.

Dad had been trying to push him out and left him for others to help when people started to arrive. Several people were on the outside pulling on his arms but he was afraid he was going to fall and didn't want to get out. It was about six feet from the bottom of the window on the lower floor to the ground because of the ditch around the foundation and I had fallen about fifteen feet from the upstairs window. My brother Neil and the community rescuers had just moved away with Mr. Jer when I hit the ground where they had been standing.

Mr. Jer had come to live with us a year or so before. Mom had taken him in rather than seeing him going to a seniors' home and he slept in a downstairs bedroom on the front of the house, facing the water.

He had been up the night before and, although Mr. Jer was feeble and needed help getting dressed and getting around, he had managed to dress himself, leave the house, and go down towards the ocean to pull up his fishing dory. He hadn't fished in thirty or forty years but had been dreaming there was a storm and the boat was going to be swept away. Mom caught up with him going towards the gate before he could cross the road to the shoreline.

Because Mr. Jer had been up the night before, Mom was sleeping lightly. She had heard strange crackling sounds and got up thinking it could be Mr. Jer again. But it sounded like fire. She called my father out of his sleep telling him she thought the house was on fire.

When they came out of their room, they went down the stairs, looked out through the living room to the kitchen, and felt intense heat. Mom told Dad to get Mr. Jer and she went up to wake all of us even though there was no evidence of a fire, just the heat, and no smoke to be seen.

They called to my brother Eddy on the chesterfield and told him to go outside in case there was a fire. Dad went in to Mr. Jer's room on the right, closing the door behind him. Once he had roused Mr. Jer from his sleep he opened the window in the room but Mr. Jer would not get up nor would he go out.

Since he was older and had mobility issues Dad told me later he wanted to get him out first, thinking he would have lots of time to go back for everyone else. He wasn't aware that after he closed the bedroom door, and as doors and windows were opened or broken out, the fire had become very aggressive. The old, dried wood in the house's structure and the tarpaper and oil painted panelling did not take long to be incinerated. While he thought he had lots of time he literally only had very few precious minutes.

Mom had gone into our room and shouted for us to get up, loud enough for everyone to hear her. She could hear the crackling noise get louder and the smoke filled in quickly. She thought we were awake and told me that I spoke to her although I cannot remember that because things were hazy when I woke up.

She went back to the hall continuing to shout for us all to get up and come to her room where she would make blanket ropes to get us out. The door had almost closed behind her as it always did when she went in and, with her back to it, she had no way of knowing how terribly quickly the house had turned on us all. When she opened the door again to see where we had gone, she was met by flames and jumped out through her own window, ropes forgotten, to see if she could help from outside, hoping we would all be out and be safe.

As Dad tried to get Mr. Jer through the window, one of the neighbours, Mike Tremblett, who had been going fishing with his son, saw the smoke and came to help. Another neighbour, Ben Power, further down the Harbour, saw the smoke and got his wife to call people to help as he raced up through the Harbour with the horn blaring on his truck.

As Mike and others showed up, Dad realized that he had no time; he jumped out the window ahead of Mr. Jer, took the ladder off the fence and brought it around to the porch. Since the porch was now all in flames he continued around the house to his own room in time to see Mom dropping from the window. She got up off the ground and ran for the corner of the house where she thought Dad might be just as I landed at her feet. By this time the house was engulfed and a ladder would do no good so Dad abandoned it. There was no way back in.

When I gathered my wits about me, with adrenalin flowing and a few breaths of fresh air, I scrambled up from the ground and ran several feet to a grassy knoll near the road. I rolled around several times in the dew-dampened grass to relieve the heat that was scorching my body.

I was lucky I had gone to bed the night before in just a cotton bra and panties. School had closed for the summer the day before and it was very warm that night, too warm for my flannel nightgown. I wasn't a bit self-conscious about all the people seeing me in this state of undress – at any other time I would have been mortified.

When I got up out of the grass my mother was rushing towards me with several neighbours. People were crying, shouting and panicky and saying I had to get to the hospital.

The "Shop" was the natural gathering spot to make arrangements to get to the hospital in Placentia. It was a grocery store owned by Josephine (Jose) and Sebastian (Seb) Walsh who were good friends of the family, and in the small community of 150 or so residents everyone was a friend. I don't remember getting into a vehicle but me and my mother did and made the one minute drive down the road away from the chaos.

There were more cars and trucks coming towards us with horns blaring; sounding the alarm that something was terribly wrong in North Harbour. Otherwise the morning was tranquil, without a ripple on the ocean; the sun had just risen and the sound of the vehicle horns could be heard close and in the distance. I turned and could see people running into our meadow and we passed several people on the road hurrying on their way to help.

At Mom's brother's house, my uncle Dick (Richard) Power was up to go fishing when he looked out, hearing the horns. He called his sons and they rushed through the door and saw the smoke somewhere up the Harbour. They had no vehicle and ran towards the scene. When they got to the top of the hill that obscured their view, they were able to make out that it was our house on fire. They watched the destruction play out as they neared. When they made it to the meadow they learned that not everyone was out.

As we got to Jose's they were up and getting dressed because of the noise of the horns and the phone ringing. Although the Harbour stretched out along St. Mary's Bay and most of the houses could be seen from further down the Harbour, a small hill hid our house from their view and they didn't know what the ruckus was about. When Jose saw me standing there, the whole household was put on alert. They knew I needed immediate medical attention and maybe the rest of the family did as well.

Placentia Cottage Hospital was the closest, about an hour away over dirt roads that weren't the best at the best of times. Seb drove a double-cabbed, light blue Chev pickup and said he would take us, and knew we had to go in a hurry. My brother Neil had arrived there close behind us.

Jose scrambled to find something to put on my mother's feet and gave her a pair sneakers belonging to one of her boys. I refused to put on anything and continued on in my bare feet.

As we made our way down the front steps of the house attached to the store, I was wobbly but said I did not want anybody to touch me.

Mom got in the front with Seb, and me and Neil scrambled into the back seat of the oversized cab. Jose offered me a blanket; I shook my head. She put it down on the leather seat to mask its coolness.

Everyone was getting ready fast and urgently discussing who else needed to go. Jose told us to go on and they would make sure whoever else needed to go to the hospital would be taken care of. Whoever else was coming would meet us at the hospital, but we had to get going.

I was glad to be breathing fresh air again and starting to calm down. I realized that my heart rate was getting back to normal, no longer pounding uncontrollably in my chest.

I sat on the edge of the back seat as we proceeded back up through North Harbour. When the truck reversed out on the road and turned to go towards the house I could see the smoke and flames in the distance over the small rise in the road. Our home was almost all red flames and the black smoke painted a bleak contrast on the clear blue cloudless sky. As we neared the now crumbling fiery skeleton of the structure, Seb stopped for my father, who got in and put his arms around my mother and held her as she silently wept. We sped off towards the hospital.

I could make out what looked like people trying to form lines with buckets of water but it was futile. They began to worry about the houses next door, several hundred feet from the fire. Most of the fishermen in North Harbour, who had been up for a day on the water, as well as their families, arrived trying to save whatever and whomever they could. The Volunteer Fire Department was several communities away. They had been called into action but had not made it yet and would not make a difference from what I could see. The provincial forestry truck had also been called because it, too, had a pump to direct water at the debris.

The conversation in the truck concerned whom we saw outside and what had happened. I didn't do any talking but I listened to Mom and Dad, Seb and Neil as they spoke about which family members each other had seen. Nobody was really grasping the ramifications – if you weren't out, you weren't getting out. They talked about seeing Eddy and Larry, and had heard that Richard was out as well, although neither of them had seen him.

It was a forty-five-minute drive to Placentia when the dirt roads were good and Seb was doing his best to beat that record even though the roads were soft and full of deep potholes. A moose jumped out as we sped along and Seb had to stop and wait because the animal would not let us pass for what seemed like a long while. Neil wanted to get out and throw rocks and make noise to get it off the road; however, Seb kept blowing the horn and gradually it wandered away as if there was all the time in the world. This slowed us down by five minutes or more and Seb tried to make that up the rest of the way.

As I sat on the edge of the seat trying my best to balance on the bumpy dirt road, I held my arms up in the air and out from my shoulders because they were starting to sting and ache. I concentrated on rocking back and forth, front to back, in order to get some relief from the nerves that were firing all over my body. Neil constantly asked me if I was alright and I would nod that I was.

As I assessed what I could see of myself, I noticed the skin on my fingers and hands bubbled out so I held my fingers apart. It was like there was a plastic see-through glove covering my hands, held in place only by the fingernails, which had turned almost greenish-black. My face was stinging, my arms were hurting and my muscles ached as I continued to rock to and fro concentrating on the movement to relieve the pain. I never made a sound.

We were silent for the last half of the drive as reality slowly crept in. I could hear the rattle and bang of the truck as Seb tried to navigate around the potholes. Mom was buried in Dad's arms and I didn't realize that her arm had been cut on the glass of her window, creating a huge gash above the wrist, and was bleeding profusely. She had her arm wrapped in a sheet that served as a makeshift bandage trying to stop the bleeding but it wasn't much help.

As we got nearer to Placentia, each of us was lost in thought, trying to make sense of what had just happened.

When Mom had realized that it was real, that the house was on fire, she had gone to make a rope out of bed sheets for us to get out, thinking we would follow her into her room. She couldn't see us through the smoke and fire when she tried to go back into the hall and didn't comprehend how much the fire had progressed because her door had automatically closed. There was nothing else she could do so she smashed the glass and lowered herself to the ground through her window. She wanted to get Dad to help us all from the ground, and was thinking maybe he had done this and we were already out.

She said she thought she heard Barry shouting out that he couldn't see; I never heard anyone except for my mother calling us, and of course, saw Larry when he came into the room. Neil was across the hall from their room and never heard Barry either.

When Neil woke up he was groggy – Larry and Richard were out of bed ahead of him and Larry put on his jeans while Richard took the time to put on all his clothing, including jeans, shirt and sneakers. Neil was a bit behind them and by the time he hauled on his jeans both brothers had already gone from the room.

Neil tried to leave moments after them and as he was going out the bedroom door he said a huge "hand" of smoke and fire seem to suddenly bat him in the face and knocked him backward onto the floor. As he lay there choking on the smoke and fire that had gotten into his lungs, he believed that both brothers would be outside by now and that he had to get out, too. He never saw the conditions beyond the door because he had been blocked trying to leave.

Before he could get up off the floor, Larry was back in the room again – unknown to Neil, I had gotten Larry to go back from our room only seconds before. Neil got up and both he and Larry opened the window in the room and took turns taking breaths of fresh air as the smoke escaped around them. Neither saw Richard after he left the room.

While Neil was outside the window for fresh air, Larry broke the glass in the windowpanes on the top and tried to get his head out as well. The glass spilled down on Neil's bare back but fortunately never cut him. They both knew they had to jump even though there was someone directly below their bedroom window trying to get Mr. Jer out. Both scrambled out the window, dropping to the ground below. Neil helped get Mr. Jer away from the house as sparks showered down on him and the rest of the people who· were arriving to help.

Eddy was still trying to find a way to get back in through the porch on the rear of the house until it eventually collapsed. He was frantic, not knowing who was in or out, and remained there from the time Dad showed up with the ladder until long after the police and forestry personnel tried to get him to leave.

The Linehan property on the morning of June 19, 1980.

In the truck, Mom looked back at us several times and told me later that she thought I was covered in cobwebs. She couldn't make any sense out of how that had happened and she didn't realize the extent of my injuries.

As we made our way through the streets of Placentia to the hospital I felt myself getting weaker – the adrenalin was wearing off, my body was starting to shut down and I was getting weary.

When we got to the back doors of the hospital – the ambulance entrance – Mom, Dad and Seb got out of the truck cab and hurried inside to get some help for me. Dad looked back and told me to stay where I was until somebody came for me. Neil stayed with me in the back seat.

The three of them went up the ramp and disappeared into the cottage hospital. It seemed like they were gone forever although it was only minutes. I felt like I didn't have much time – I didn't know really what that meant but I felt compelled to get help while I could still stay on my feet.

I asked Neil to let me out of the truck as my hands were no longer working inside the bubbled skin. He came around the cab and opened the door and tried to help me down. He couldn't find a place on me to hold so I slid out of the truck and when my bare feet hit the gravel I pushed myself upright and walked toward the ramp with the last bit of strength I could muster. My legs were burning from the inside because of the position I had been sitting in and the stones beneath my bare feet pinched as I headed towards the ramp. Neil hovered in case I fell but didn't touch me. It had suddenly gotten very cold and I started to shiver.

As I stumbled up the ramp it was getting harder to breathe. Neil opened the huge metal door and I walked in on the second floor of hospital – the ambulatory clinic. When I got inside there were several nurses running towards me with a gurney. One of them told the others to lay me face down on the stretcher.

The stretcher was lowered enough for me to let myself fall forward. I pulled my arms into my sides as gravity took me down to the bed. My skin felt like it was cracking and breaking as I moved. My energy was gone. I was wheeled off to a room where there were lots of shiny metal sinks, metal bowls, and rolls of bandages. I didn't know where my parents had gone as they were nowhere in sight.

I had made it to the hospital but I felt myself fading fast. I didn't think I had any more to give.

When we left North Harbour there was already a lot of activity in many different households. Some people had rushed up or down through the Harbour to see if they could help.

The police were on the way, and the local volunteer fire department and the people from the forestry unit were called in from Mount Carmel. A group of firefighters were also dispatched from the Kenmount Fire Station in St. John's and from Whitbourne. Later, fire investigators showed up along with more police officers to determine what happened that morning.

At my aunt Marg and uncle Dick Power's house, Marg got on the phone and started calling for help, not really sure at first whose house was on fire. She called the parish priest, Father Val (Valentine) Power who also had to come from Mount Carmel.

When Father Power got to North Harbour he quickly assessed the scene of the fire and proceeded to Marg's to find out what had happened, who was gone to the hospital, and who needed to be notified. By this time the understanding was that there were four dead in the fire.

Father Power called my sister Mary in St. John's and told her that the house was gone and four of her family members had died in a fire. Mary dropped the phone in shock and ran to her room howling in tears.

Her roommate picked up the phone and Marg came on the line and told her what had happened and she got as much information as she could before hanging up and going to help Mary. A priest from St. Theresa's Parish had been dispatched to their apartment to be with Mary while she made arrangements to get home, and he arrived a short time later.

Mary was devastated. She couldn't remember much about the next several hours with the exception that she called a friend, Kay Boland, to bring her as far as Mount Carmel where other friends, Bertha and Richard Fowler, would bring her home.

Meanwhile information and rumour seemed to point to the fact that one more person was unaccounted for. Father Power asked Marg to check around to be sure that we were all home that night. Some thought Francis might not have come home as he and Eddy had been out the night before, some said they saw Richard or heard that Richard had been out, and back at the scene investigators only had four bodies.

After making calls and finding out that, with the exception of Mary, we had indeed all been at home, the priest relayed that information to the investigators. They went back for another search. An hour or so later they found Barry. Because he was so young and so small it had been very difficult to find him in the burned out remains of the house.

Marg called her daughter, Marie, who was also in St. John's, and she came home with Mary, although Mary never remembered that. The whole drive out Mary was under the impression that four had died, while Marie knew the difference but did not know how to tell her. When they got to Mount Carmel, Mary's friend gave her the news that five had died and that I was gone to the hospital but nobody knew how I was.

Mary doesn't recall much after that, except for walking from my grandparent's house in North Harbour, to stand in front of the graveyard looking over at the total destruction that had been her family home, while investigators sifted through the remains.

Father Power also went to tell my grandparents that their grandchildren had died. That, too, was a difficult visit.

My aunt May (Mary) and her husband Cecil Critch also had to be notified of the tragic events. Father Power made that early morning call to St. Mary's and mayhem broke loose in that house as well. All May's family were home for their eldest son Cecil's induction ceremony that would take place on the 21st. He was taking his final vows to join the Christian Brothers. Mom called Cecil the next day, Friday, and told him to go ahead with the event, and he did as she wished although he always regretted not postponing it for later.

Our whole community, along with many more communities in the bay, were in a state of complete and utter shock. Parents were waking their children on the first day of summer holidays to tell them that their cousins, friends, neighbours and classmates were gone. The media got hold of the story and the news spread throughout the whole province and beyond.

Both my uncle's house and the Shop and many other places in the community were filled to capacity over the next several hours as people from neighbouring communities showed up to see how they could help.

Eddy stayed at the scene and refused to leave. He waited until everyone was accounted for in the ruins. Despite my uncle Dick's pleading with him not to look and other friends asking him to leave, he insisted on seeing each body before they were brought away. The police officers complied.

Eddy had not seen me at all but had heard somebody say that I was seriously burned. He couldn't comprehend what that meant but pictured that I would be similar to what he had just witnessed and that was not good.

In the hospital, as I weakened, I didn't really grasp what was going on around me. My parents were gone somewhere in the building and there were masked faces hurrying everywhere – one of them I recognized as Dr. H. Ross Penney, our family doctor.

It was strange that he was in the hospital at this hour since he only did clinics at the pharmacy up the street during the day. I later learned that somebody had called ahead to tell the hospital that we were on our way in. Since the hospital staff didn't know how many were injured all the doctors in the area had been notified to come help out.

He asked me how I was doing as he and the nurses worked to soak bandages in sterile water and layer them over me on the stretcher. I could see them in the hazy reflection of the bowls and sinks that were in my line of vision, working with speed and efficiency. They placed what felt like hundreds of bandages and I could feel their weight and coolness as they were layered on, one strip over the other, across my body.

I heard the doctor mention that there was a gash on my lower back but that it had burned closed. Somebody lifted my left arm and removed the watch that I was wearing and gently laid my arm back on the stretcher. The watch had burned on to my arm and the hands had stopped at 4:46 am, June 19th.

My strength was leaving me and it was a chore to even speak. Once they had finished applying bandages, ambulance personnel came to take me away to St. John's where the hospitals were better equipped to deal with my injuries. The doctor gave the paramedics and an accompanying nurse a case of the sterile water and instructed them to keep pouring it over the bandages so they wouldn't dry out. After the doctor finished working on me he went to see to my parents.

As I was being wheeled down the hallway back towards the ramp, Neil came to the stretcher and bent low to ask me how I was doing. I squeaked out, "OK," asking, "Mom and Dad?" and he said they were fine as the stretcher moved on.

Before getting to the door the stretcher stopped again and the parish priest, Father Dermot McGettigan, from Placentia rushed in. He said some prayers over me before continuing on to be with my parents. Later I learned that he had given me the sacrament of Last Rites.

During the ambulance drive I could feel myself getting weaker, which I didn't think was even possible. I could feel the life slowly draining out of me. The siren was blaring and the nurse and paramedics were talking in hushed tones as we sped towards St. John's. Occasionally the nurse would pour water over me and I could hear the splashes and feel the cool water. The nurse also had a jug of ice water and a straw that she put to my lips whenever I moaned to let her know I was parched. I was so thirsty by now I couldn't get enough.

I tried to turn my head and move around to be more comfortable but movement was too exhausting so I gave up in an effort to save my energy. Time seemed to stand still; it was about an hour's drive from Placentia to St. John's, but it seemed like we were driving forever.

I knew when we were getting closer because the driver was speaking to somebody on the radio. I could hear part of the conversation from the dispatcher who was asking how I was. The nurse spoke in low tones to the driver to update him on my condition.

The dispatcher told the ambulance to take me to the Health Sciences Centre (HSC), which was not their original destination. I was only fifteen and the age limit for the HSC then was sixteen so I should have gone to the Janeway Children's Hospital. However, the HSC was closer and would save fifteen minutes driving time. The nurse felt there was such urgency to get me to the closest hospital that extra time was the difference between life and death.

Beneath me, I could feel the ambulance maneuver through the streets of St. John's and then there was a sharp turn, the siren was turned off and the doors in the back of the ambulance flung open. I was very cold by now, and the 7am air made me even colder as it penetrated the wet bandages.

As I got bumped and pushed out of the ambulance and into the hospital there was a flurry of activity all around me. Orders were shouted, and facemasks and green gowns were everywhere, even more than there had been in Placentia. They moved me from one stretcher to another and as my pillow was changed I could smell the burnt flesh that remained on it and it nearly made me sick.

Although I was aware of what was going on, I didn't really absorb it. I heard them talking about trying to get an IV into me but there was so much swelling it seemed impossible. I was catheterized at some point but couldn't remember when it happened. The bandages applied in Placentia were carefully peeled back and the doctor, who I later learned was Dr. Ken Anderson, tried to assess what he saw.

My body was burned from the mid-thigh upward in various stages of first, second and third degree burns with my arms, chest and back getting the worst of the damage. My mid-length dark hair had been burned at the ends and what remained was matted with smoke and scorched hard edges.

Green-clad people, who I assumed were doctors, tried to get an IV in somewhere; I could feel several sets of hands moving over my body trying to find a spot for the needle. I was turned over so that I was now facing up. They gingerly checked my forehead but that was ruled out. I heard somebody say that this was it, if a vein couldn't be found in my ankles there was nowhere else to look. Too much time had passed from the time of the burn and my veins were collapsing.

I felt my left ankle being poked and prodded before the searing edge of a blade cut through the skin, and after several attempts the IV was unsuccessful. Dr. Anderson took over the right foot and I felt my ankle being twisted and strained, then the searing edge of the blade again, a cut, and some pressure as the needle was inserted. There was a collective sigh of relief.

Somewhere in the crowd of green gowns and facemasks, I heard somebody say in a hushed tone, "Make her comfortable, she won't make it through the night."

At fifteen-years-old I felt the surge of a stubborn streak that didn't surface too often and I said to myself, *Oh yes I will, just watch me!*

I was in Emergency for what must have been hours as they started to clean me up and the hospital prepared a "Burn Unit" on the fourth floor. In 1980, this Burn Unit was only erected when the need was there, and today – June 19th, 1980 – I was that need.

In Emergency they started to remove any skin that was hanging off. I opened my eyes as my hand was lifted and I saw a green figure peel the skin from my hands by squeezing tweezers near my wrists and lifting the skin and pulling it back. It was like removing a large plastic see-through glove as the skin turned wrong side out from my wrists to my fingertips. If I didn't see it come from my hand I would never have believed it. It didn't hurt and I could feel my other hand being lifted on the other side of the bed, undergoing what I guessed was the same procedure.

Some, but not all of the black smoke was cleaned off me before I was finished in Emergency. With so many open wounds, there was too much of a chance of infection so they wanted to get me out of there as quickly as possible.

I heard somebody say to take me to the elevator to the fourth floor. As I was wheeled through the halls of the HSC towards the elevator I became anxious. I had never been on an elevator before and I wasn't sure if I would like it or not – if it was dangerous. With all that was going on with me, I was afraid of the elevator!

As the doors closed I was nervous and was glad when they opened and I could be wheeled out. Quickly the stretcher moved to 4 North A, room 4272, where the Burn Unit had been cordoned off from the rest of the hospital. A number of nurses met the stretcher as I was pushed through the outer doors leading to the readied Burn Unit. I said, "I know what happened," to nobody in particular as I was moved further into the room. This would be my home for the next number of months – if I were to live. Very quickly and with great efficiency, I was transferred to a bed, face down again. Monitors were hooked up, bags of IV were running freely through my body, bells and alarms were set up and a nurse took up residence beside me on a chair. At some point she was joined by Father Joe Barbour who had been our parish priest in Mount Carmel and was a friend of the family.

I could hear Father Barbour saying prayers over me near my head and I concentrated on his voice. Nurses came and went, changed IV bags, administered drugs, and did other nursing duties making sure I was still alive. Father Barbour never left my bedside and continued praying. I could hear the drone of his voice and it was somehow soothing. Sometimes it trailed off when he was either tired or thought I was gone so I would try to move my head or make a sound and he would start praying again with renewed energy.

I closed my eyes, concentrating on his voice, and every now and again I would open them to make sure that I was still alive and he was still there. His eyes were closed and I could make out beads of sweat on his shiny forehead as he continued to pray in hushed and hurried tones.

For many hours this was how it was. When I felt my body try to slip into nothingness I would open my eyes for just a second or concentrate more closely on his voice and try to stir my body so he and I would know I was still there. *This is me – Ida – and I want to live.*

"He who has a why to live can bear almost any how."
~ Friedrich Nietzsche

Time passed. I didn't know if it was day or night or how long it had been since I was moved to the Burn Unit. I didn't sleep but I guess I must have gone in and out of consciousness and my mind was empty of all thoughts. The nurses came in and administered morphine or valium at specific intervals. This activity made me more alert and then my body would be freed from pain. A nurse continued to stay in the room and Father Barbour was still there, deep in prayer with his head bowed.

I could hear one of the nurse's voices talking to me and asking questions about how I was doing, but I was unable to answer. She told me that everyone called her "Rusty" because of her red hair. I could tell by the laugh lines visible above her mask that Rusty (Tibbo) was a pleasant person and her kind tones suggested she would take good care of me. I tried to smile but it was impossible to even do that. I felt bad because, growing up, we were taught to respect our elders and not responding was not respectful. I hoped I would be forgiven.

I heard a team of doctors, including Dr. Anderson, come in and he talked to Rusty about my catheter and she said that there was nothing. My kidneys had shut down and almost fifty bags of IV fluids had gone into my body. Although some of it was escaping through wounds, my kidneys were slowly poisoning me and I had gained significant weight from the fluids and the trauma.

Dr. Anderson consulted with his team and told the nurses to prepare me for surgery as they had waited as long as they could and I would now need dialysis immediately. I believe that at first they had thought that I wouldn't make it long enough for the kidneys to complicate matters. Now they were trying to give me every chance I could get. If I were to survive, the kidneys had to work or I had to be put on dialysis. This is what I understood from the conversations, even though it was mostly medical jargon and they were speaking very low.

Father Barbour had to leave the room as the team of nurses prepared me for surgery but he continued to pray even as he was going through the door.

The nurses gathered on both sides of the bed and grabbed onto the edges of the blanket that I was laying on. They picked me up using the blanket and moved me to the stretcher for transport to the operating room. I was lucid but my body was not responding to any commands I was trying to give it – I wanted to assist myself in moving but my muscles would not cooperate. I was lethargic, in a state of what I figured must be near death; however, the activity around me told me I was still alive.

As they were setting me up on the stretcher with IV and fixing the monitors I heard Rusty shout out to the doctor. He came back in the room and she showed him the catheter bag – it was starting to fill up. I could sense a change in the room, an excitement. Between the clapping and sighs of relief, Rusty bent low to my face and whispered, "Good girl." I tried to smile but was unable. I didn't know what I had done to deserve the compliment, but I was happy for whatever I had accomplished.

The doctor patted my foot as he went round the bed and told the nurses to put me back and get ready to clean me up. His tone suggested that I had made some sort of turn for the better. *That's good*, I thought, *that's good!*

Once I was put back on clean sheets on the bed, nurses worked on me for the next few hours. They brought bowls of water and bandages and proceeded to clean my face and body. I could tell there were still remnants of smoke and tar because of the smell of burned flesh that was in the air whenever I was moved.

Several times I asked myself, *Is this a dream?* and *Will I wake up soon?* I still couldn't take in what had happened because such tragedies existed only on television and not in real life.

Rusty came in and out of the room and talked to me like she was chatting with an old friend. Although I could only see her eyes, she reminded me of my mother and that was comforting. She wiped my mouth inside and out with a cotton swab that was dipped in a sweet liquid. This would keep my mouth moist but my tongue and throat were too swollen for me to do more then make a croaking sound, and even that was exhausting and painful.

I thought back to all the sore throats I had had in the past. Nearly every Christmas and Easter, when all the family were enjoying the treats like apples, oranges or grapes; and sometimes a chocolate marshmallow Santa or bunny depending on the occasion, I had to leave mine until I got medicine because I couldn't swallow. Although they were extremely painful I had learned to wait those out – count the time between swallows, tell myself it would not be much longer. That is what I would do now – wait out the pain and count the time between swallows.

As the day progressed I became more aware of my surroundings and although I was hurting, I didn't make a sound. From what I could hear in the hushed drone from the nurses' station outside my door, it sounded like it was the morning of June 20th and more than a day had passed since the fire.

I thought of my family – I had never been away by myself before so I was starting to feel a bit homesick. Myself and Sharon had stayed with Mom's sister, aunt May, in St. Mary's for a few weeks the summer before, but because Sharon had been with me that was different. I was alone here; I didn't even know where Mom and Dad were, or where anyone was.

I thought of the conversation in the truck on the way to the hospital and I knew the home I was missing and the family I needed wasn't the same, and never would be again.

The bag at the side of the bed was emptied many times over the next few hours. By later that day I began thinking about the situation between needles of morphine pushed through my IV. I knew I was alone in the Burn Unit because the door was slightly ajar and all efforts were concentrated on me. I knew Sharon had been with me in the house and, from the condition I was in, I knew if she wasn't here, there was no way she had made it out, it would have been impossible.

Sharon was dead!

This thought was so unbelievable that I got mad with myself for even thinking it at first. But the more I considered it, the more it became true: I resolved myself to the fact she must be gone. I didn't really fathom at this point what it meant that she was dead, but I knew that she was dead none the less.

I thought some more about the drive to Placentia. I knew that Richard and Neil slept in the same double bed. Neil had said he thought he saw Richard outside or heard somebody say he was outside but he wasn't sure. Neil knew that Richard had left the room before him and assumed that he could possibly have been out.

Dad said he had not seen him so I figured from the direction he had come from, Richard must have been the person I banged into in the hall, and he couldn't have gotten out. The fire was raging by that time and there was no getting down the stairs.

There was no talk of Barry or Harold either; they were the youngest boys – aged ten and twelve. If they were in the yard I would have seen them because they would have been looking for Mom or Dad. They couldn't have gotten out. Francis, who was twenty-one, slept in that same room and would not have left them behind. That was the room where I had broken the window with my fist and I could not see anyone there. They must have still been in bed and perhaps were overwhelmed by the smoke before I got there. Things had happened so fast!

Eddy also slept in that same room but often stayed on the chesterfield downstairs and he was sleeping in the living room that night. Dad had called to Eddy as soon as he came down the stairs and said they thought there might be a fire and to get out. Eddy felt an unusual extreme heat but he did not see any flames. He ran outside through the porch almost on autopilot. When he got outside in the fresh air he realized almost immediately that the house was on fire because it was climbing the clapboard. I believe that some of our heads must have been muddled with carbon monoxide and the fresh air helped reverse whatever confusion it caused. For those that were not lucky enough to have a breath of fresh air, I believe the smoke and carbon monoxide cocktail would have complicated matters for them. Dad had said Eddy was out so I knew he was out and had tried to get back to help us, and I hoped he had not gone back in.

Eddy could not get near the house in those few seconds; he burned his hands and singed his hair as he tried. He ran down to the pile of wood that Dad had left to dry in the meadow, picked up a few pieces of chopped firewood, came back to the porch and threw the wood at our bedroom window in an attempt to wake us, not knowing we had already left the room.

If he was seriously hurt he would have been here at the hospital too, but I hadn't heard anything like that.

Larry had been in our room and I knew he was up out of bed and I heard a nurse in Placentia say that somebody was bringing him to the hospital when I was leaving in the ambulance. He had had a seizure shortly after getting out. I knew he was alive and if he was "burned-hurt" he would be here close to me; since he wasn't and it was the next day I believed that he was OK. If he had had a seizure while in the house he would have never made it.

It was almost incomprehensible how quickly things had happened. I was probably less than a minute behind Larry in the hall and those few seconds had been the difference between life and death for some of us. As I really started to think about it, I didn't like the picture that was forming in my mind.

From what I could tell Sharon, Barry, Harold, Richard, and Francis were dead.

This had to be a dream! I was only speculating because there was no way this could be true – surely somebody would tell me. Then again, maybe somebody had and I didn't remember.

Maybe there were more! Mom or Dad hadn't come in.

Maybe something bigger was wrong – if that could be possible.

Maybe I was the only one left.

I didn't want to ask the question out loud because I knew I would not like the answer. I wanted to keep the hope alive that I wasn't entirely alone.

Instead, I kept thinking, *If this is a dream, somebody please wake me up now!*

Maybe late Friday or what could have been the next day or day after, I was upgraded from critical to serious condition. That must be good, I figured. I could hear Rusty at the nurses' desk tell somebody on the phone. She talked about me in some detail before hanging up, and then made her way towards my room. I could see her approach through the slight crack in the doorway. She pushed open the heavy oak door to tell me that Mom had phoned.

That meant I wasn't alone!

I was so happy and I croaked out a "thank you" sound and tried to smile. I was getting really anxious to see a familiar face and couldn't wait until my mother came to see me. Maybe she could tell me it wasn't real.

I didn't know at that time that my mother had been kept overnight at Placentia Cottage Hospital and she hadn't realized that I was taken by ambulance to St. John's. Nobody had told her in Placentia that I was sent on because they could not help me at the Cottage Hospital. The doctor wasn't sure that I would even survive the trip so he didn't want to give her hope. It wasn't until she went to North Harbour late the next day and I wasn't there, that she found out I was in the Health Sciences Centre.

Mom still didn't know the state I was in when she called and could not comprehend what it meant, whether I was critical or serious. The last time she had seen me I was sitting in the back of Seb's truck and I was alert and talking.

While she was at the hospital she had a visit from a friend from Placentia who was going out to see what was going on. Mom told her to go see my grandparents to check on how they were and come back and tell her. Along with all of us, she was also terribly worried about her parents at this time. She thought the news would kill them.

She wasn't concerned about herself at all and tried to direct her concentration on how others were doing.

As the day progressed I could feel myself getting a little bit stronger. I could turn my head from side to side and I tried to look down at myself but all I could see were white bandages and the bed sheet. My arms were too heavy to move but as far as I could tell they were still there. I wiggled my toes and saw the sheet move to correspond with the action. That was good. A team of nurses came in for me and said I had to be put in a bridine (iodine) bath so that some of the dead skin could be removed and to get rid of the smoke from my skin.

The bathtub was directly across the hall from my room. I could hear the water running into the tub as a nurse approached with a wheelchair.

It took about a half an hour to get me ready to get out of the bed. All the bandages that were not stuck on had to be removed and thrown in the garbage; the others would come off in the bathtub. The nurses again positioned themselves on either side of the bed and grabbed onto the sheet to move me. With practiced ease they successfully placed me in the wheelchair.

As they wheeled me out of the room I noticed the mirror above the sink was covered with paper; although I didn't question it at the time I wondered at the reason.

At the bathtub the nurses again positioned themselves to hoist me from the chair into the tub. I noticed the water was orange and bubbly and Rusty said it was the bridine to ensure it was safe from germs.

I was lowered under the water, the bandages were given a few minutes to soak and then a nurse on both sides of the tub used tweezers to tug and pull to try and remove them.

I watched the water turn red as my blood mixed with it. I could feel the pinch and sting as my skin was torn loose with the bandage.

The moist air in the bathroom helped ease the dryness in my mouth and throat. I was still on IV and wasn't allowed to have any food or drink so that was welcome.

The nurses took both my arms and started to tug on hard, dry, black skin with the tweezers to remove it. At first I thought my skin was just dirty from the smoke but as they talked I realized a black thick leathery coating had formed on my arms.

One of them told me they wanted to get at the pink skin underneath and that I would do this every day until all the black was gone. My right arm was the worst; it looked like a piece of burnt roast and I could faintly see the blood running underneath some of the skin in places between the black.

Dr. Anderson came in to examine me and he knelt down by the side of the tub. One of the nurses asked him if I would be going to Boston for treatment. He looked straight at me and said absolutely not, that he was going to keep me there and that I would get better under his care. I could tell he was smiling under the facemask and I recognized his eyes from the Emergency Room when I was brought in.

He spent some time going over my injuries and gave some orders to the interns that were with him. He talked about a number of surgeries that would need to be done and described them in medical terms that I couldn't understand.

From what I could tell from the conversation, I believed that the surgeries would be complicated and risky. He asked Rusty if they had parental consent for surgery and she replied that it had been verbal over the phone and that it would be in writing when my next of kin came to visit in the next few days.

He turned and spoke to me again and told me not to worry, that I was in good hands and that he would take such good care of me I wouldn't want to leave. He patted the top of my head before he got up and left.

Rusty took his place on the side of the tub and assured me that he was the best possible surgeon I could get and that I would be fine. She said if I had not gotten Dr. Anderson that morning in Emergency, I might have been sent to the Shriner's Hospital in Boston. She also said that they would take as good or better care of me right here on this ward.

After what seemed like hours in the tub being picked and scraped (they called it debriding), it was time to be moved back to bed. The nurses folded several soft blankets to get me out of the tub and tried to place them under each arm so that they wouldn't damage the skin any further.

I noticed that there were only three places on my arms that were not burned – directly under my armpit (so Rusty told me), a spot the size of a dime at the bend in both my elbows and the mark left by my watch. Everything else on my arms was burned to varying degrees.

I couldn't see much else but the nurses had been using tweezers to pick at my back and my chest to remove some of the black skin so there was damage there as well.

If this is a dream it is time to wake up, went through my mind again and again, and it did so for the next couple of weeks. Although I knew deep in my heart that it wasn't a dream, I tried to keep the hope alive that it was, and that my family and I had been spared.

When I was back in the fresh clean sheets of the bed, I was coated with a cream on my face and body and then I was bandaged up again. This took hours as each finger had to be done separately, then my arms, my body and neck and lastly my face.

I tried to be like a rag doll so the nurses could move me in whatever direction they wanted and I would be less of a burden to them. I was a very accommodating patient and throughout the next several months the doctors and nurses continued to tell me this.

When I was settled after the bath and bandages I was so exhausted that I just lay there staring at the ceiling. But sleep eluded me. Drugs were administered and the IV bags were changed fairly often.

When Rusty was there again and after she had moistened my mouth with a wet swab, I finally asked the question that was playing on my mind. I asked her if my family was downstairs. She told me that they would be in after a few days.

I managed to say, "Rusty, that is not what I mean; I mean is my family that were burned downstairs." She said that I was the only one with injuries.

I said again, "Rusty, I mean the ones who died, are they downstairs?"

Rusty realized what I was asking and she replied, "Yes," in a hushed voice.

I hoarsely said, "Thank you for telling me," and she left the room.

I had seen enough of the news on TV to know there was a morgue in this hospital and if there were dead bodies they went to the morgue. It was comforting in a way to know they were here close by even though I knew they would never be with me again.

It finally started to sink in, that this was it, and it was real. I was in for the fight of my life, not because I didn't want to die but because I didn't want my family to hurt any more than they already must be hurting. I couldn't be selfish and give up because it would be so easy to do that. However, I wasn't raised to be a quitter. I hadn't quit in the house, and I wouldn't quit now.

At first I didn't know what time of the day or night it was, but shifts changed because I would see new eyes behind the masks and would hear different voices. I really liked the shift that Rusty, my mother figure, was on.

No matter what time it was, the nurses noticed that I was always awake; I had not slept to any degree since I was brought in to the hospital. If I slept I thought I would die and I could not do that to my parents.

My cousin Gerard Critch came to visit and I knew why he was there. He talked about the fire and proceeded to confirm what I already knew – Sharon, Barry, Harold, Richard and Francis were gone! I never shed a tear; it was as if he was telling me a sad story.

Although it was my family he was talking about, it was not real for me.

I asked him questions about the funeral and what was going to happen – again without any emotion. He talked about how the funeral would be outdoors because the church in North Harbour was too small for the crowd that was expected.

I asked him if he could take pictures for me so I knew what was happening. He said he would.

After Gerard left I thought about my family again and especially about Sharon and Harold and Barry. We were so close and usually travelled in what I sometimes referred to as a pack. We mostly stayed together and played together in our own meadow. If we went to the Shop, we went together and I, being the oldest of the four, always had the sense that I was "looking after" them. That would be no more. I was the new baby in the family.

More drugs were administered and the lights were dimmed for the night.

I couldn't sleep and I still didn't cry. I tried to think about how things would change for me and my family. I thought of Mom and Dad and what they must be going through right now.

I don't know how much time had passed as I lay in the hospital bed wrapped in bandages but, incredibly, Sharon came there. She was standing by the side of the bed and was smiling at me. I asked her how she could be here, and said that this must be a dream.

She assured me that it was not a dream, that she had come to tell me she was OK. She knew I would be worried.

My surroundings were strange; it was like the hospital bed had been transported to our bedroom at the house and the hospital bed was our own bed and I lay there bandaged. She was standing by the bureau in our bedroom and she had a slightly surreal glow about her.

Again I said to her that this must be a dream or caused by the drugs but she said that it was not. Sharon said she didn't have much time but wanted to come to see me before moving on. I asked her what she meant.

She said that she came back to thank me for trying to save her but that it was her time to go and she was not scared and had suffered no pain. She told me when she died she had gone to a "holding place" and she would stay there for what would be a few weeks in our time. She said that I wouldn't understand but that was the best she could do to describe it.

I asked what she did in this holding place.

She said it was a place where the girls went when they died and that Francis, Richard, Harold and Barry were in a similar place for boys. She said after a few weeks in this place they would all be put together where they would no longer be girls or boys but would just be themselves, their spirits. She told me not to try to understand it but just to know that it was a good thing, that it was a really nice place, that she was not afraid or lonely and that she was fine.

Sharon was still standing by the bureau in our bedroom and I wanted to ask her so many questions. She said she didn't have much time, that not too many were granted access to their loved ones but because of our strong bond and my age, she was allowed to come for what would be a few minutes for me.

I still couldn't believe she was there. I said, "Sharon, this has to be a dream."

She told me to stand up and I could stand and my bandages were gone. She said to put my arms around her and hug her. I did and she hugged me back, I could feel her. She said, "In dreams you can't feel anything;" she asked if I could feel her. I hugged her tighter and sobbed because I could feel her arms comforting me and the warmth of her flesh.

Then she said she had to go, that there wasn't much time.

"Sharon, I really need to see the others. Is there anything you can do?"

She said that they were in a different part of heaven and it wasn't that easy but she would see.

I let go of her and within seconds a black pipe-like hole appeared by her side. That is the best way I can describe it. It was like looking into the mouth of a huge black tunnel. She said that this was the line to the "boy side" and it was the best she could do, that they couldn't come here. I could see clearly through the round tunnel to the other side even though it seemed like a long distance from where I was standing to the other end.

At first I could see sunshine on a grassy field and wild flowers, then Barry came into view and said he was alright and not to worry. Harold was next to appear at the end of the "pipe" and he said the same thing. All I could see was their freckled faces and red hair and they were smiling. After that both Richard and Francis came into sight and said they were OK as well. Again I could only see their faces and they were also smiling. I told each of them that I loved them and would miss them and would think about them every day and they told me the same thing.

The pipe-like hole disappeared from beside Sharon and she said she had to go. I asked her to hug me again to make it real. As I stood there in front of her, she grabbed on to me and gave me a big bear hug and said that I would be fine. She asked me not to forget her.

"Never!" I said, and then she was gone. Suddenly I was back in the hospital room, lying bandaged in the bed. Something powerful had just happened and it gave me the strength and fortitude to fight harder to get better. I was a survivor and I couldn't forget that.

I was still wide awake and had not slept since Thursday, the morning of the fire. When the nurse came in to change the IV and administer more drugs she asked if I was alright. I told her I couldn't sleep and she asked if I would like her to read to me. I nodded and she went out and got a magazine somewhere and came back to the room. She read to me in intervals between tasks and she turned the pages showing me pictures of celebrity faces smiling back at me from the glossy pages.

By the time the shift had changed in the morning I still had not gone to sleep.

The routine had been set the day before. Removing bandages in the bed, being carried to the bathtub across the hall and "debrided," and then carried back to the room to be re-bandaged.

Dr. Anderson came and went with an entourage of interns and doctors a couple of times that day. He seemed like he was always smiling and he looked at me and talked to me as if I were the only one in the room.

There was a wire rack of clothes just outside my hospital room door stocked with gowns, pants, hats, masks, booties and gloves and whoever entered had to wear it all. To me everyone looked like the same green people; the only thing distinguishing one from the other was their size, their eyes and sometimes an escaped lock of hair. I could tell if a person was smiling by the crinkle at the corner of their eyes and by the tone of their voice.

I missed my family and familiar faces. With the exception of Gerard and Father Barbour, I did not remember seeing anyone I knew since I came in and I was feeling homesick.

This morning, once I was back in the room, the team of doctors showed up with a photographer. Dr. Anderson said that they wanted to do a study of my burns for learning opportunities for future residents and interns. He asked if I would mind. I nodded acceptance and since my bandages were off after the bath this was the perfect time for the photos. After today, I was told, the photographer might come back at various intervals of treatment over the course of my stay.

I asked Dr. Anderson how long he thought I would be staying in the hospital and he said about five to six months.

I said rather succinctly, "I will cut that in half."

He only smiled and patted my head with his gloved hand. He told the nurses that I could have some liquids to see if I would tolerate it before he left the room.

The photographer snapped lots of pictures before the nurses could start to bandage me again. I was getting cold so I was glad he was gone.

The nurse brought me some ice water and a straw. She told me to sip it slowly as she held the straw to my lips. My throat was so dry that I wanted to drink the full glass but I listened to what she said and tentatively took a sip. I could feel the ice cold liquid on my tongue and my throat and my mind's eye could trace it as it made its way to my stomach as if a cold pencil was drawing a trail.

The nurse looked at me and I smiled – so far so good. She told me she would wait for a few minutes before giving me more. I was looking forward to it.

One of the nurses brought a couple of Get Well cards and read them to me and stuck them each with a push pin on the little cork board by the window. She opened the curtains and said it was a beautiful sunny day out. She said since I couldn't sleep I might as well enjoy the sunshine. This was the first time I had seen outside since I was brought in.

Later a mild-mannered nurse named Joe who, next to Rusty, became my favourite, came to the room with some water. Joe told me he would be with me on a shift for a few days and that he had been there when I was brought into Emergency. He said he never thought I would still be here and that he was so glad that I was. When he found out that there was an opening on the Unit for a few days he had asked to come up.

He was so kind and gentle that we quickly became friends. I asked him on the second day if I could have a mirror. He asked me why I would want one and I said that I wanted to see what I looked like. He said I looked beautiful and alive and what more could I want? I smiled at him and said that I wanted to see what I looked like so I could know what kind of a fight I had on my hands. After giving me sips of water he said he would think about it for a little while and let me know.

He spoke to the other nurses outside and made a phone call, I guessed to Dr. Anderson. He returned a short time later with a hand held mirror behind his back.

He asked me if I was sure I wanted to see what I looked like. He said that I hadn't fully been cleaned up and not to get discouraged. He held the mirror up an arm's length from my face. I asked to move it closer and he did.

When I looked at the reflection I did not recognize the face staring back at me. I looked at Joe and asked, "Is that me?" and he nodded.

My face was enormous, my hair was broken off in some places and burnt off in others, my skin was peeling in some areas and had dark red blotches and sores in others. There were angry red lumps on my nose and along the lower edge of my right cheek. I looked away for a second in disbelief and Joe started to lower the mirror. I shook my head and he brought it back up again.

"Joe, tell me the truth, is this bad?"

Joe looked at me with a smile and he said, "It is right now but it won't always be like this." He went on to tell me how I had gained so much weight because of the IV and my body was hoarding the water to try and heal itself. I had been around ninety pounds when I was burned and I must be at least two hundred now. He said when my kidneys were fully functioning and the IV was removed that I would get back to my original size. He said that the skin would peel and heal on my face and some other places would have scarring but at this point it was hard to say how much.

I asked him some more questions and told him to be honest with me because I wanted to be prepared. If I felt prepared I would get better. He said he would and I believed him. He sat on a chair beside the bed and placed the mirror on his lap and talked to me for a long while in his soft patient voice about medical procedures I could expect but said that ultimately my body and my attitude could help determine the outcome.

That was good enough for me. I knew I had to fight, I had to do what I was told to do, and I had to do it with a smile no matter how hard it was.

Drugs were administered every four hours and parts of the day I was in a state of blankness. During the blank periods I did have visitors but most of the time I didn't know if somebody had been there or not. I was confused by the new cards and teddy bears that were amassing on the window ledge, sometimes not knowing if somebody had brought them or if I had received mail.

For the non-blank times, my mind wandered back to my family and friends and what they must be going through. I convinced myself that I was not in any real unbearable pain but just feeling more of a throbbing and stinging when the drugs were wearing off. I did not think of myself or what I had to go through in the coming months. I figured I would handle that as it came and adjust when necessary.

The next day was the first of many things I had to "handle."

During the daily bath a discussion arose between the doctors and nurses as to whether they would take off my fingernails or not.

I became fully alert and asked what they meant. One of the nurses showed me my hand and I could see that at the end of my burned and battered fingers where my fingernails used to be were greenish-black, spike-like protrusions sticking straight upwards from the fingers.

I could remember the doctors removing the bubbled skin from my fingers as if they were removing a glove. The nails had remained but were now not like fingernails at all. The nail beds had risen and only a tiny portion of the nails were hanging on to the fingers.

I asked what would happen if they removed the nails and I asked that they please tell me the truth no matter how hard it would be to hear.

The doctor said that if they remove the nails, I may never have nails on my fingers again. He said that they were working very hard to ensure that I did keep the fingers and that the nails might not be an issue if that didn't happen.

I said in a determined voice, "As long as I have fingers, I want fingernails."

The doctor looked at me and I could see his jaw move as he smiled beneath the mask as if to say, "Well look at you." He said if that is what I wanted they would try to accommodate unless it meant that I would lose my fingers. I was relieved.

I had a very strange shivery feeling go through me when I thought of not having fingernails. I didn't want to have that feeling the rest of my life so I was hoping that they would not have to remove them.

The stumps on the end of my fingers were not very attractive but neither was the rest of me right now so I was fine with that.

The black hard skin on my arms seemed to be growing even though the nurses were taking some off every day. It looked like a person could knock on it like they would a door; it seemed that hard. The doctor said I would go into surgery that evening or the next day and have a lot of this removed because they couldn't do enough during bath time and I was too weak to have more than one bath a day.

When I was put back into bed again I was exhausted. The effort of just being moved was great and I didn't fully grasp how sick I was until it was time to move me.

Drugs were administered, time passed and I still didn't know what day it was.

"I bear a little more than I can bear."
~ Elinor Hoyt Wylie

I heard noises from outside my door and I could see through the crack that somebody was dressing. It wasn't a nurse because one of the nurses was explaining what needed to be put on. I was anxious to see who it was.

When the door was tentatively pushed back I looked into the eyes of my mother. The mixture of joy and sadness that I felt in my heart at that time was overpowering. It was complicated – confirmation for me that the possibility of this being a dream was now over, and the joy of seeing her and knowing she was here. I forced myself to be strong and not to cry although the tears were very close.

As she came into the room she hesitated and looked around. Then she made her way swiftly towards the bed with her arms out as if to hug me. When she realized that she couldn't hug me her eyes filled with tears and she started to cry as she said, "I'm sorry" – two little words, but two very powerful words that shook me to my very core.

I had never seen my mom cry before, with two exceptions. One was the day in the truck as we were going to Placentia, and one was when I was much younger. Her cousin and good friend,

Paul Power, had died and when the phone call came to the house I remember seeing tears in her eyes before she went upstairs to her bedroom. I imagined then that she was crying but had only seen the tears for a few short seconds before she hid them and I was very young.

Mom was a very strong woman and she must have a lot of heartache and anguish for her to cry. I made my mind up right then and there that I would not cry, that I would be strong for her, and that she would not have to cry for me. She deserved the strength that I hoped I could show.

She told me later that when she first entered the room she had no idea that it was me in the bed. I was so swelled out of shape that she thought she was in the wrong room. She said the person in the bed was huge and seemed like they were covered in white paper, almost like it was a cloud. She hesitated and almost went back out looking for me but realized there was nobody else in this part of the hospital and a paper sign saying "Burn Unit" was on the double doors.

When she realized it was me, the first thought that went through her mind was that I was finished – I didn't have much longer to live. She had had no idea I was hurt as badly as I was and when she saw me she thought she would be burying another child. She was powerless to save another one of her children and that was why she had simply said, "I'm sorry."

Mom and Dad always had so much to deal with. Although we would have been considered poor, so were many other families at that time. We always had something to eat because we had vegetable gardens, hens, sheep, a cow, and Dad hunted for meat for the table. He worked in the lumber camps in Badger and was gone most of the year. Mom put in the gardens and she tended to the animals, sometimes with the help of neighbours. But times were still hard.

Dad, Edward Linehan, was born in John's Pond, St. Mary's Bay, the youngest in the family. His mother died before he turned two and his father died when he was eleven. His aunt Johanna first took care of him, and after his father died he moved in with relatives in Holyrood. Some of his older siblings left for Boston and Montreal as soon as they were old enough to go. The only family that stayed around was his sister Tessie (Theresa Trough) who eventually came to live in Colinet, the next community to ours in St. Mary's Bay.

Dad's older brother Peter was captain of a trawler (*Belle*) that went down off Boston in 1947 and all hands were lost. He also had three brothers (Paddy, George and Jim) who all drowned at a young age in separate accidents in John's Pond – two while hunting and one from epilepsy when he had a seizure and fell into the water.

Although he didn't know them, he had had two more brothers (John and Willie) who died at birth. Needless to say he was familiar with losing loved ones, if such a thing was possible.

As a young man of nineteen, Dad went off to Scotland with the Newfoundland Overseas Forestry Unit during the Second World War – he was one of the first to enlist and remained there until the war was over. He never talked much about his time there. When he returned from Scotland he started working in Badger. He met and married Mom when he was thirty-six and she was twenty and they settled into life in John's Pond.

Mom, Catherine (Power), was born in North Harbour, the youngest of four children – Frank, Dick and May all being older.

Most of my older siblings were born in John's Pond before the family was resettled to North Harbour. Dad bought an older bungalow in North Harbour so we could have a place to stay. He then took apart our two-storey saltbox house in John's Pond and marked each board and rebuilt it in North Harbour. The older house was torn down and the land was plowed off directly in front of the rebuilt house, which left the ground rocky. We moved in when I was five or six years old.

Hardship seemed to follow my father and mother. Mary, the oldest, named after my father's mother, Mary Theresa Nash from Branch, St. Mary's Bay, and my mother's sister May, was sick from birth and after many trips to the Janeway she was diagnosed with celiac disease and was allergic to infant formula. Special milk had to be ordered and it was very expensive. She was sick almost all her young life and at one point the doctors thought she had leukemia.

I remembered one time when Mary was a teenager she had gotten two teeth pulled at the dentist in Placentia. The next morning I woke in a pool of blood and screamed for my mother. Mary had almost bled to death right there in our bed and had to be rushed to the hospital. That was how it was with Mary.

Eddy was born eighteen months later and was named after my father, and Dad's father. Francis came along another eighteen months later. He was named after Mom's older brother, who drowned when he was twenty, and her father.

Francis had severely deformed club feet and was in the Janeway Children's Hospital for months after he was born. He had many surgeries and was in and out of casts and on crutches until he was fifteen. Mom made numerous trips back and forth to the Janeway with him.

Neil was the next oldest and born a little over a year later. He got sick when he was a teenager and had a severe kidney defect and had to have one of his kidneys removed. This was almost un-heard of in the 1970s and there were many trips to the Janeway. In fact he had his appendix removed and almost died during that surgery before he was correctly diagnosed.

The next year Richard was born and, similar to Francis, he had club feet and was in and out of casts and special boots for many years, well into his teens. He was named after Mom's brother, our uncle Dick.

Larry came along almost two years later and from an early age he was diagnosed with epilepsy. For years he had multiple seizures a day until he finally had brain surgery, which was semi-successful. Larry had a hard life and was bullied because of his illness. He often came home with large bruises because of falls that came along with the seizures or from punches or kicks that accompanied the bullying. Larry frequented the hospital probably the most out of us all.

He had fallen in front of cars, off scaffolding, in the yard, in the house, on the bus, in the school: it was a regular occurrence for him to have a seizure and it was a normal part of our lives, as strange as that may sound.

Because of his seizures Larry found it hard to make friends. People were afraid of the disease. He spent a lot of time around the older people in the community because they accepted him as he was.

I was born two years after Larry; then came Sharon, Harold and Barry. Barry, too, had club feet and was in casts and special boots off and on for several years.

My first recollection of Barry was when he was six months old and Mom laid him in my arms as I sat on the daybed in the kitchen. He had shiny red hair and a beautiful freckled face. I was around six and he was so heavy because of the huge white casts on both legs. He too had a lot of surgeries in his young life.

I remembered Francis, Richard and Barry with the casts that sometimes had a bar between them, or special boots that some-times had a bar between them and other times with walking casts. It was part of who they were but I never once heard any of them complain.

While Dad was away working in Badger, Mom had to look after the household and made many trips back and forth to the Janeway with several children at a time. Finances were non-existent. Mom often told us of the times she had to go to the hospital with three or four children and would leave the house before six in the morning and get home long after dark on the taxi and would not have enough money to even get a cup of tea for any of them.

Sometimes the appointments would be so long that the taxi would leave without her and she would have to stay overnight at her mother's sister's house – our aunt Annie Dalton. Mom was forever grateful for aunt Annie who was always good to her and always welcoming. While Mom was gone, my grandmother would stay with the rest of us. I was named after her, my mom's mom – Ida Power.

If there was such a thing as a God-given right to be depressed, either of my parents could qualify. They both had had a hard life. But neither one complained nor felt they were overburdened – at least from what we could see as children. We always felt loved.

All the regular childhood illnesses that came along – measles, mumps, chicken pox, etc. – Mom handled them ten at a time, and never once did I see her overwhelmed. She was a rock.

I swore that day when I saw my mom cry that I would not make it any harder on her, Dad or anyone if I could help it. She would not know if I was in pain because I never wanted to see her cry for me. I would be resilient like she was.

Mom asked me lots of questions and I assured her I was fine. I asked about her arm because I could see the bandage. She said it was a scratch and a few stitches although I knew it was more than that.

I didn't dare ask her about the funeral because I didn't know if it had happened yet but I asked how everyone was doing. Mom said everyone would be out to see me soon. She stayed for a little while just staring at me and occasionally attempting to touch me but she was hesitant. I told her I knew I looked awful because I had seen myself in the mirror but I told her what Joe had said and how things would get back to normal pretty soon.

My voice was hoarse but I managed to talk quite a bit to her to let her know I was doing fine.

One of the nurses came in and said that I needed to have a bath and my bandages changed. She explained to Mom that I needed to have the dead black skin removed and that I would be in the tub and getting new bandages for about two hours.

I tried to assure her that it didn't hurt at all although it sounded bad. I told Mom she didn't have to stay because I would be very tired once I got back. Her eyes watered as she touched my head and I could see her anguish. Again I told her not to worry, that I would be fine. I tried to perk up and look as strong as possible so she could see I would get better.

The nurse told my mother that she needed to sign some papers for treatments since I was underage. We talked for a few more minutes and then more nurses showed up saying they had to get me ready for the daily routine.

Mom leaned down and kissed me on the head through her mask. She told me she loved me and I told her I loved her too and not to worry about me.

I watched as she went through the door and towards the desk to sign the papers as the door slowly closed behind her. She came into view again as she took off her gown and the entire garb she had to wear – booties, a hair covering, gloves and a facemask.

She looked through the seam in the door to catch my eye and

waved at me. I smiled and I could hear her sob as she left the Burn Unit. She could never stand to see anyone doing anything with me, even for them to take off a bandage. She could handle it herself but not for me.

I was overwhelmed with sadness but said nothing, nor did I cry. It was time to be strong. If I had learned anything from my mother it was that. I would make her proud.

My cousin Gerard came in to see me again later that day. He asked how I was doing and I asked about my mom and dad and the rest of my family looking for more details. I also asked if the funeral had happened yet. He said yes, that it had been the day before. I asked him to tell me about it.

The funeral was larger than anyone could have anticipated or even imagined. They were expecting hundreds to come but in fact thousands did (an estimated five thousand).

Gerard told me how it was held outdoors and that it was a very sunny day. Cars were parked on the ocean side of the dirt road and on the inside almost in the ditch for several kilometers on each side of the church. People walked for up to a half an hour to get to the site of the Mass, which was held in a meadow not far from the church.

Our house had been built a stone's throw what we called "up" the Harbour from the church and graveyard. An excavator had removed the burned-out ruins of the house but the blackened ground and freshly turned earth was visible and stood out as a reminder to what had happened. Not that anyone needed a reminder.

A single massive grave had been dug near the fence in the graveyard closest to our yard where the house had been burned.

The unopened coffins were kept in the small church until the Mass, then they were carried over the road, passing by where the house had been and into a meadow on the hillside.

Some of the younger ones – Barry who was ten, Harold who was twelve, and Sharon who was fourteen had been carried by teachers from Our Lady of Mount Carmel High and Elementary School. Richard, nineteen and Francis, twenty-one, had been carried by family and friends.

At the top of the meadow there was a huge dark grey rock where a makeshift altar was set up for the Bishop Alphonsus Penney and the many priests performing the Mass. The coffins were brought up over the grassy hill towards the rock for the Mass. The land sloped away so that everyone could see the proceedings.

People gathered around the makeshift altar, behind to the woods, down into the five-acre meadow and out onto the road. The single road in the community was almost impassable.

Author photo

Lucy Fogarty's meadow, site of the funeral Mass.

Once the Mass was over, the coffins were brought back to the graveyard to their final resting place. The Bishop said prayers over the grave and my mother told me much later that when the coffins were lowered into the burial place there was a mix up in the order. They were not lined up in sequence by age and Dad wouldn't have it. He got down in the grave and fixed the layout, aligning the upper end of the coffins before allowing any clay to be spread on his children.

Because it was a Catholic Mass and it was Sunday, a Funeral Mass was said on Monday. Father Power, our Parish Priest, said that in the church and the building was blocked. It was only years later I learned that my father was not at that Mass; he had taken ill and was at the hospital in Placentia. He had a severe inner ear infection and had lost his eyeglasses in the fire, leaving him disoriented. He was dizzy and nauseated for a couple of days before finally having no choice but to go for help when he could no longer function and began falling around. Mom was tortured because she kept telling him that people would think he was drunk and neither one of them knew what was wrong with him. He was kept in the hospital for a few days to give him time to recover physically and emotionally.

I could picture many of the people who might have been at the funeral. For the last several years, as my older siblings attended college or worked in St. John's, they would bring home any number of friends. Some were from the Northern Peninsula, the West Coast or the Burin Peninsula and couldn't get home until Christmas or summer holidays.

The visitors enjoyed the lifestyle of the bay and Mom's homemade bread and a cup of tea right from the teapot. The house was bursting at the seams almost every weekend. Beds were crowded with three or four people and other beds were made up on the floors. It was commonplace to have twenty or more people in the house on the weekends – and for sure every weekend that had a holiday

Monday in it. Mom or Dad never cared how many came and never said "no" to anybody. Our home was always welcoming. Dad would joke that it was a steady stream of tea and toast every morning.

All the communities on either side of North Harbour in St. Mary's Bay, in Placentia Bay and in Trinity Bay probably gave a good showing as well. There would be a lot of classmates and former classmates there for sure. Most people around North Harbour were interconnected through family and friends, or through the school system, and others genuinely wanted to show support. I was happy there was a big crowd; they deserved a good send-off.

Gerard said he had taken pictures that morning but did not have them developed yet. I told him I still wanted to see them and I thanked him for doing it because I knew this was not easy for him either. Again I was very clinical about the whole experience. Although I knew it was real I was still hoping it was a dream – that I would eventually wake up.

As he was leaving somebody else was coming to fit me out for casts or plastic splints, at least that is what one of the nurses told me. I was apprehensive. The only casts I had ever seen were on my brothers – Francis, Richard and Barry – bulky, heavy, white monstrosities.

Joe came in with another man and a cart full of materials that were wrapped in dark green cloths and he explained what would be happening with the castings, which they called splints. In order to keep my fingers and hands from curling up and deforming they were going to be making moulds of my hands and each day these moulded casts would be bandaged on to my hands after my fingers and hands had been dressed separately. The bandages would help cushion my hands and a layer of cotton batting would be placed on the mould to make it more comfortable.

I watched as the orderly poured boiling water in a bowl and cut a sheet of hard beige plastic into a huge mitten shape. He laid my bandaged hand on the shape and made a few cutting adjustments. He put the mitten into the boiling water for several minutes.

He placed a couple of blankets and plastic bags on the bed under my hands. He used tongs to clasp the plastic and curved the edges upwards where my wrist would be and folded the thumb downward so that the plastic was more of a hand shaped object. He dried the plastic and placed it under my bandaged hand. The mould hardened and kept this shape until it was heated again.

He continued this process, plying and shaping the object, until the plastic was like a fitted mitten for the bottom of one hand and partway past my wrist. Then he started the process again and made one for the other hand. Once I was fitted out, these casts were firmly attached to my bandaged hands with another layer of bandages. The casts extended out beyond my fingers by a few centimeters to protect the tips of my fingers and to keep everything in place.

Joe said these would remain on my hands anytime the hands were bandaged, that it was important if I wanted to keep them structured as they were supposed to be. It was not any more uncomfortable with them on so I didn't make any protest.

When they were gone, the nurses fitted me out with sheepskin booties to protect my heels on the bed (they had already put a sheepskin blanket beneath me the day before). My heels had begun to get sores from resting in the one place so long.

The call button was pinned on the pillow near my head. This was a red button attached to a long cord that plugged into the wall. If I needed assistance I had to push that button. Since the nurses were with me most of the time this button was not a priority, but when I needed less care this had to be considered.

I was getting used to the daily routine, and then it was Thursday – the one week anniversary of the fire. I was terrified the whole day and especially that night – I can't begin to explain why but I was anxious and frightened, of what or whom I did not know.

The nurses told me at different times that I seemed really quiet and sad but I insisted I was fine. As the day passed and the night came, I couldn't stop myself from reliving the fire over and over again in my mind. It was like a movie on constant rewind.

I tried to figure out what I could have done to make things come out better to make a happy ending. It was no use. (Neil told me later that no matter what we did differently it might not mean the ending would be changed, just the steps leading up to it.)

When I became agitated, the nurses took turns and sat with me several times to see if I would sleep or get some relief, but I couldn't and didn't. They tried talking to me to engage me in conversations but I was quiet and nothing would chase away the terrifying feeling that was building inside me. I couldn't explain what was wrong because I didn't know.

One of the nurses called for the doctor on duty who came round well into the early hours of the morning and prescribed something to calm me down. After 5am the feeling left me and I was back to myself. I wondered what had happened and what was wrong. I hoped the next night wouldn't be the same.

The next morning I was unwrapped again and Dr. Anderson came in for rounds. When he saw my chart he asked me what had happened the night before. I explained that I was terrified for some reason and it wouldn't go away. He said it was probably aftermath of the trauma and that my mind was catching up to my body's experience.

Dr. Anderson came back again when I was in the tub. He was very concerned because the dark black skin was invading my arms. He told the nurses to leave me longer in the bath and see could they get some extra black skin taken off.

He checked my fingers for gangrene and said although they looked alright at the moment he was probably going to schedule surgery in the next day or so. When I looked at my fingers I did not see "alright" but I trusted him.

I told him that I was hungry; I had not eaten in over a week and this was the first time I had the hungry feeling. He said that was an excellent sign and that I could probably have a broth later that day and maybe then my IV would go if I could keep down food.

Mary came to visit that day for a little while. She was very sad when she saw me and cried a lot. I asked about everyone and she told me about how things were going. She was more interested in me and wanted to know if there was anything she could get for me. I told her I couldn't have any food but she got a glass of ice water and helped me with the straw while she was there. It felt good to get more water into me and I was getting hungrier now.

Visitors were only allowed to stay a short while so that I wouldn't be tired out. She told me she would be back again the next day and kissed my head before she left.

Mary was ten years older than I was and had gone off to high school when I was very young and then to college and work. Even though she was only twenty-five she had been home mostly on weekends for the last number of years. Mary lived in St. John's now and her daily visits would be a welcome part of my routine as the days passed.

On the rare occasions that Mary went home for the weekend I missed her visits. She was great company and she usually brought others with her to read to me and to just be there. All my other visitors found out that I liked the McDonald's milkshakes and some days I drank three or four. I loved them and people were so nice to bring me a treat.

My IV was removed seven days after I was admitted to the hospital and I was allowed to eat and drink. I never liked the hospital food as I had grown up on meat and potatoes and home-made bread. I had little in the way of an adventurous spirit for anything else so I hardly ate a thing. Mary came by every evening and now that I was able to have food she brought me a McDonald's strawberry milkshake as well as a plate of homemade fries. She heated a package of turkey and gravy that came in frozen packs from the supermarket when she got there. It was so good and she must have gone through almost a hundred packages that summer.

I began to get a few more visitors as each day went by. Some people that I had never met before but who were friends of my parents came by to see me. One of my cousins brought me an autograph book after she saw all the cards that were amassing on my walls and said to get my visitors to sign it. I got nurses, teachers, friends and family to sign the book when they came in.

My hair was growing and the burned edges were getting in my eyes. One of the nurses arranged for a hairdresser to come in and cut off the dead ends to make it easier for me to see and for them to keep it clean.

The nurses got me out of bed and put me in the wheelchair before my bath without taking off any bandages. They covered me in several sheets as if to make a tent and only my head was left out. They taped garbage bags around my neck to make sure that no hair would get into my bandages or, more importantly, into my wounds.

Once I was ready the hairdresser came into the room dressed in all the garb required of any visitor. My hair was course and thick and sometimes I would say I had "horse hair" on my head. I told the hairdresser and she laughed and agreed with me.

I heard the snip of the scissors and saw pieces of hair fall all around me. As she started to cut I could see the dark, dead knobby-burnt ends falling on the white floor. She sprayed my head with water several times to keep it wet so that she could get all the bad ends out. By the time she finished my hair was extremely short but she said it was a lovely style. I trusted what she said because I didn't have a mirror to look at myself. My head felt lighter though and I was glad for that.

The hairdresser was very nice and talked to me the whole time she was cutting my hair. I thanked her several times and she said it was her pleasure. She told me where she worked and said she could come back if I was here for any length of time.

It took a lot of my energy to sit there so she finished as quickly as she could, and although I was tired I still had to get in the tub.

The nurses rolled the wheelchair away from the hair, brushed me off and removed the garbage bags. When they got to the hallway they started to remove the sheets and by the time I was in the bathroom getting ready for the tub, I was naked except for the bandages. I could hear the double doors open and close and a vacuum cleaner start up.

When Dr. Anderson came he called me his beauty. He winked at me and said he loved my new haircut. I told him I had the latest style from all the best salons and he laughed.

But as he looked at my arms he was not pleased. I could see it in his eyes. This couldn't be good. He said he would monitor it for a few days but he felt I would need surgery sooner rather than later.

When I finally got back into the bed I was exhausted. I was almost asleep as the nurses bandaged my arms, but sleep eluded me. It was discouraging to be so tired just from doing simple things. I hoped at some point I would get stronger.

Two days later, I went to surgery for the first time. My arms were slowly being taken over by the black hard skin and no matter how long I stayed in the bath, the nurses could not keep up with the growth. The longer baths were tiring me out and no ground was being gained.

The nurses started to remove my bandages again. The ones that were stuck stayed on and would be removed in the operating room. I didn't pay any attention to them as they were busy working on each side of the bed: "un-mummying" was becoming a common occurrence.

My mind was on my parents and hoping that they would be alright if something happened to me in surgery. My mom had given consent for the surgery the evening before. She would never get over it if something happened and she had given consent. I knew she was no longer as strong as she appeared. She was keeping up for me and me alone. My being burned was a distraction from the depths of despair and I was glad that I could be that for her and my father. She wanted to come to see me before surgery but Dr. Anderson knew how far away it was and said I would be going in early and would not be awake for most of the day. He told her to wait. As my thoughts came back to my room, the IV was attached to the shunt that still remained in my ankle. I was lifted in the bed sheet to the stretcher. The monitors and catheter were transferred to a mobile pole to accompany me on the journey. I had to go to the second floor, which meant the elevator again. I still wasn't sure if I liked the elevator or not so I was a little anxious about that again.

The nurses put a huge white sheet over me, covering everything except my eyes. They said that since I would be going through the corridors they wanted to make sure I was protected from germs.

The trip was short as I was very near the elevator. I watched the lights overhead as one passed, and another came into view. I was on the elevator, off the elevator and being pushed through the big double doors of the operating room (OR) rather quickly.

There were many doctors and nurses there. I recognized Dr. Anderson by his eyes and his voice as he welcomed me. He said I had to speak with an anesthesiologist about the surgery after he explained what he would be doing.

I asked him to be honest with me so I knew what to expect. I was nervous and intimidated by my surroundings but I tried to be brave.

Dr. Anderson told me that my arms were covered in the hard dark skin which needed to be removed and since there was so much of it and it was growing so fast the daily bath wasn't helping.

He placed his hand on my head as he continued, and said that my right arm was the worst and he wasn't sure if he could save it below the elbow but that he had every hope that he could. He said that the black skin could lead to gangrene which could mean amputation so they had to deal with it swiftly.

He explained that once the black skin was removed they would have to replace it with good skin taken from my thigh. He told me not to worry, that he had every expectation that everything would go smoothly and that I would be back in the Burn Unit within a few hours.

He talked for another little while about the procedure to the doctors and then he left the immediate area to prepare for surgery with the usual pat, this time on my foot, as he was going.

He was then replaced by another doctor who said he was the anesthesiologist. I asked what that meant and he said that he would be with me all the time monitoring my vitals and that he was the person in charge of putting people to sleep. He mentioned that they were trying out a new drug on me and instead of going to sleep I would be in a state of paralysis and that I wouldn't know what was going on around me. I would not hear sounds or be able to turn my head or make any movement. He said this was safer than being put to sleep and it was not as traumatic on my body and my organs.

He asked if I understood and if I was OK with this new drug.

I told him I had never been in surgery before so if he, being the expert, was fine with it, then so was I. But deep down I was petrified.

He told me what would happen and how the drug would be administered via the existing IV so there would be no more needles.

Dr. Anderson was back and leaned over the operating table. He nodded around at each of the others assisting and told me who each one was even though I only saw their eyes. They each said "Hi" or "Hello" as Dr. Anderson introduced them. Then Dr. Anderson said that they were getting ready to administer the drug to put me out.

I was nervous at this point but I knew it needed to be done so I nodded and watched as the doctor pushed a needle into the IV line. Within seconds my throat felt dry and I lost all concept of time and space. A huge set of lights was moved over me and I could see the lights and looked at them for what must have been hours. My mind seemed like it was semi-alert; however, I had no feeling and was unaware of what was happening around me, just as the doctor had explained.

After a very long time, which I couldn't measure in hours or minutes, I started to hear sounds; faint at first but then they got louder. I could feel pressure on my arms and my right leg. I could hear instruments clanging and banging and voices that were low and droning but I could hear them. The lights that I was staring at overhead came into sharper focus.

I didn't think that this was right and wanted to let them know that I was awake, but I couldn't make a sound. I tried several times to call out but my voice was stuck somehow. I felt a burning sensation at my leg and I jumped a little. I felt a hot searing pain on the side of my right leg and a sound must have come out of me. There was a flurry of activity and I saw a plastic mask come towards my face and the anesthesiologist was there as the mask lowered over me.

Everything went black.

I opened my eyes and looked around. Rusty was there and she said, "Oh, so you decided to wake up, sleepyhead!" I had no idea how long I was out but I hadn't slept in so many days there was a good chance it was a long while.

Rusty made her way towards the bed and said I had her scared for a little while and she had been trying to wake me. I was back in the Burn Unit and there were beeps and noises coming from monitors all around me.

As Rusty looked down at me I could see she was smiling by the way the mask moved around her face and by the laugh lines crinkling at the corner of her eyes. She asked me how I was doing and I tried to speak but couldn't. She wiped the inside of my mouth with a moist cotton swab and told me not to worry. The back of my throat hurt; this was a new hurt.

She said the surgery had gone on longer than planned, that the skin was unusually tough and took longer to remove than they first thought. She said that the original drug had worn off and that I had to be put to sleep so the doctors could finish the job. I nodded that I understood but I was groggy, my head was fuzzy, and my mouth felt like it was full of cotton balls.

I noticed that my hands and arms had way more bandages on them than had previously been there. But on a good note, I had both my hands, which counted for something. My right leg was throbbing and felt really sore, then again so was the rest of me. I was a bag of aches and pains.

Rusty said now that I was awake they could give me some more drugs and she pushed a needle full of liquid in the IV line. Within minutes the aches and pains were almost gone and I was in a state of nothingness again.

I never slept much that night either although I was unaware of anything around me. As the shift changed in the morning I felt a bit better and more alert.

I tried to assess myself again. I was lying in a more upright position than I had been before. My arms were up on pillows and I tried to wiggle my fingers a little but only managed to barely move them. At least I could feel them. They were firmly encased in the splints.

Every time I tried to move it felt as if my skin was bursting and cracking so I had to do it very slowly and gently. There was a large bandage around my leg, starting just above the knee, and tracing the lump under the sheet it seemed to go up my right side almost to my waist. It was interesting because that bulge was not there before and must be where the doctor had taken the skin for grafts.

The nurse came in again checking the monitors and lifted up the sheet to look at my leg. I noticed spots of blood coming through the white bandage but she didn't seem to worry about it.

She said all had gone as planned in the surgery and the doctor was very pleased with the outcome. She said there would be no bath today and Dr. Anderson was on his way up. I didn't know whether that was good or bad.

A few minutes later he walked in the room with his usual crew. He was smiling and said he was happy with how things had turned out. He talked to the interns in medical terms I couldn't understand, telling them what he had done and how the surgery went. Then he turned back to me.

He told me that he had to take a lot of black skin from my right arm if he was going to be able to save it. The damage was deep so he took great care in order to be sure he got it right. He said because of this extra time, the drugs that had put me out were just about worn off. When I jumped on the table they had almost finished harvesting skin for skin grafts and the instrument had cut my leg. I received seventeen stitches but luckily they had enough skin by this time that they didn't have to go to the other leg as a donor site.

I had lost a lot of blood because he had to go deep in my right arm. Since it wasn't replenishing he had to give me a couple of bags of blood. He pointed to the IV pole and sure enough there was a bag of blood and a bag of clear solution.

Dr. Anderson told the nurse that an order had already been submitted to have my blood checked every couple of hours to see how the levels were. He said that the team would look at my arms the next morning but that the skin graft site would have to remain bandaged for a week to ten days. He asked if I had any questions but my mouth was so dry I couldn't talk and only a squeak would come out.

He told the nurse that I could have a few sips of water and, depending on the blood levels and how I tolerated the water, the IV might come out soon.

Since there was no bath that day the nurses had a bit more time to spend with me. They decided to work on making the call button function for me. They devised a plan whereby the button would be attached to the footboard on the bed and if I needed help I could use my feet to press the button. We tried it a few times but I couldn't maneuver my left foot to push the button and I couldn't move my right leg because of the bandage.

Next they thought about putting it on the guard rail on the bed near my feet. The rail almost went the entire length of the bed so the furthest end of the side rail was near my foot. They tried attaching it there and it worked. I was able to hit the button with my left foot and sound the cry for help should I need it.

We practiced a few times to make sure it would work. The nurse hit a red button on the wall to tell a voice on the other end what they were doing. She told me that the red button on the wall was connected to the same alert as the button on the end of the wire now attached to the bed.

The person from the lab came by several times that day. He took blood from my feet to test and sent the results to Dr. Anderson. One of the nurses came in when the bag of blood was gone and said that the doctor felt I did not need any more. This was good and hopefully meant I was healing.

I was able to get some more water down and my throat felt much better.

Mom came in to see me early the next day and again she was very upset although I am sure she was trying not to show it. I could see the tears pooling in her eyes even though they never spilled forth.

I was going to be strong no matter what and she would never know if I was in any kind of pain. I couldn't add that burden to her because she had so much to deal with.

She visited for a little while but then Dr. Anderson came in. He smiled and told my mother I was an excellent patient and I was doing very well although she might not think that I looked like I was. I was grateful he said that because he reinforced to her what I was trying to convey.

After a few minutes he got down to business and said he wanted the bandages off my arms. I thought this might be painful because there was no bath today. The bandage on my thigh was huge and couldn't be wetted and Dr. Anderson didn't want my arms to be waterlogged either. He said he would be back in about an hour if the bandages could be off by then. Then he bid goodbye to Mom and left the room in a hurry with all his interns behind him.

The nurses told Mom that they really had to get me unwrapped and that she could stick around and come back later. She said she couldn't stay and quickly kissed my head as she raced out the door.

I asked when I would see her again and she said she hoped to get back in a few days. It was over two hours travel and she didn't have a vehicle, she depended on rides from others and there were very few vehicles in North Harbour at that time. Today one of the neighbours had an appointment at the hospital so she managed to get in to see me for an hour or so.

A long time later I learned that my mother could not handle the doctors or nurses touching me in any way. She always thought they would be hurting me and she couldn't bear to have me in pain and she knew that I was. She tried to escape the room before the nurses started working on me and in her hurry she also forgot she had on the entire hospital garb.

The next thing she knew she was crossing the hospital parking lot with mask, hair covering and booties when somebody she knew from a neighbouring community happened to be going into the hospital at the same time. He recognized her and called out her name several times and chased her across the road to see what was wrong. When he grabbed her she realized what she was doing and where she was and went back to the hospital to meet up with her ride and remove the hospital clothing. She said if he had never stopped her she didn't know where she would have ended up that day.

Meanwhile, as the nurses began working on each side of me I felt like I was a mummy. There were so many bandages and they kept unwrapping and unwrapping to get to me underneath. They removed the splints which had been placed on me in the OR and when they got near the skin they slowed down to make sure no damage was done. One of the nurses got a bowl of warm water in case some of the edges needed to be soaked.

I waited in anticipation to see what skin grafts looked like and to see how much black was gone from my arms. But when the bandages were finally off I couldn't move my arms enough to see what they were like. They both felt like dead weights because they had been resting high on pillows overnight. A pins and needles tingling started to break the numbness as the arms came back to life.

Dr. Anderson came in dressed all in green and proceeded to examine his handiwork. As he lifted my left arm I could see most of the black was gone and there were several patches with lots of stitches. My arm was blue and red from bruises and burns and dotted with little black stitches. It looked like a patchwork quilt.

I asked what they were and he told me that the skin grafts had to be held with stitches to make sure they didn't move. As he came around the bed to look at my right arm he was very careful to lift it without twisting. He said we had to be very cautious with it as the skin was very fragile at this time. I managed to catch a glimpse of what he was talking about and noticed that the skin was torn and jagged. There were many more stitches on this arm. He said the blackened skin was much deeper here and some of the flesh had torn away when they were trying to remove the bad stuff. Luckily they were able to graft it and if the grafts took hold my arm might be saved.

This I took to be good news even though I could have thrown up when I looked at my arm. The flesh looked mangled and I could almost see blood running beneath the skin. For an instant I felt like crying but then I told myself that I was lucky to be alive and I would take this as it came to me. I thought of Mom and Dad and knew that I had to be strong for them and there was no room for self-pity if I wanted to get better.

My nails were still hanging on and I was happy about that. Maybe I would be lucky and they would survive. They looked horrible but they were fingernails.

I was bandaged up again and this would be the routine for the next number of days.

After a long and tiring day, the nurses came in and settled me again for the night. The lights were dimmed and the door was left slightly ajar. I lay awake again for a long, long while.

I must have dozed off for a few minutes because I came to my senses with an internal state of alarm. I wasn't sure what was wrong but I had the overwhelming sense that I was dying. It is strange to try to describe but on the inside I felt something was wrong. I didn't know what it was but I did know that I was dying. There was no doubt in my mind.

I called out to the nurse in my hoarse voice but there was no answer. I might be dying and felt I was alright with that but there was no reason to die alone. I called out again but I saw no movement in the hall through the crack in the door. It must have been really late because the hallway was in semi-darkness as was customary at night. My room was dark except for the moonlight flooding in through the window and the dim light shining in through the nearly-closed door.

I waited a few seconds and called out again. I was alone in the Burn Unit as there were no other patients in the cordoned off area that made up my space. Still no answer! The overwhelming sense that I was about to die grew stronger inside me. This wouldn't do, I was not afraid to die but for some reason I wanted to have company when it happened. That was foremost in my mind.

Then I remembered the call button that had been readied at the end of the bed. Although I had never used it, I had practiced and it wasn't hard so I moved my foot around a little to see if I could raise the alarm. It wasn't at the side of the bed on the end of the rail in reach of my left foot so I moved my foot around exploring the bottom of the bed. There it was on the footboard. I could feel it on my toes and I tried to curl them enough to push the button on top of the call bell. As I made a little push the casing gave way and I could hear the sound of plastic hitting on the hard tiled floor. The noise was deafening in the quiet room. Now what was I going to do?

I tried not to panic as I called out again, this time in a louder voice. I waited and waited and never got an answer. So this was it, I was dying and dying alone! I was determined not to let this happen.

I contemplated my situation. The call button was attached to the wall on the left of the bed and I was attached to a lot of wires and tubes on the right side of the bed. I knew the call button could be triggered on the wall as I had seen the nurses hit it many times as they tended to my wounds. If I could only get to the button on the wall I could alert somebody to my predicament and I would not have to die by myself.

I hadn't been up walking since I came in but I knew if I had to I could manage it. The sheepskin booties around my heels and ankles might be slippery, but if I was careful I was sure I could walk. I was going to give it a try.

My arms were too heavy to move because they rested on top of pillows above my body and felt like a dead weight. I dragged them one at a time off the pillows partially by willing them to move and partially by maneuvering my shoulder. I watched as they plopped on the bed by my side.

The pain I felt then was extraordinary. It felt like the skin had burst and broken on my arms but I couldn't see blood, at least not yet, and I did not feel any wetness beneath me. Maybe if I stayed there for a little while the pain would subside, but the sense that I was dying was growing stronger and I was still alone. There was no time to wait; nor to waste.

My arms were of no use to me because they were numb and heavily bandaged, but I had my head and my legs. I tilted my chin as far up in the air as I could manage and I dug the top back of my head into the pillow beneath. I wiggled my head enough to knock the pillow away and pushed it to the side. I tilted my chin again toward the ceiling as much as possible and dug in my heels at the bottom of the bed. I pushed with my head and pulled with my heels and, sure enough, I moved down in the bed a few inches. I couldn't bend my legs very much because of the bandage from the graft site so this was going to take a little while.

There was a bedrail on each side of the bed, ending below where my knees were, so I knew I had to get further down than the bedrail in order to get out. I worked and worked at digging in my head and my heels until my heels reached out over the bottom of the bed. The sheepskin booties helped cushion my feet against the hard wood of the board and I could get a little bit more traction as I pushed and pulled my way down.

The bandages around my body began to bundle up on my back and pulled on my front, almost strangling me. I didn't know what damage I was doing but I had to get out of there.

The top of the bed was raised a little so when my head reached the bend in the mattress I figured my legs could clear the bed rail. I still felt like I was dying and my concentration on moving my way down the bed had eased it a little but not all the way. I swung my legs upward and to the right knowing I was running out of strength and if this didn't work I would probably be found like this when the nurse came back.

As my legs swung upwards and gravity pulled them down and out over the side of the bed my body came upwards and rolled so that I had done a complete turn and my feet were on the floor and my head was face down in the bottom of the bed. I had gotten this far, wow! I was almost there.

I waited for the pain to settle in my leg where I had rolled over on the bandaged area. Then with one big push off from my forehead I managed to stand up on the floor. The sheepskin booties helped keep me from going backwards and landing on the window ledge. I stood there trying to keep my balance as my body acclimatized itself to standing upright.

I was in a tangle of wires and tubes but I didn't care as long as they didn't trip me. I pulled myself away from the bed with the sense that I didn't have much time growing more alarming inside me. As I took a step around the bed I pulled the IV and the catheter out because they were caught in the bed rail and the stationary stand at the head of the bed. I had to get to the call button.

As I took the few steps around the bottom of the bed my energy started to fade. I came round the end of the bed where there was a chair between me and the wall so I had to be careful of that in the semi-darkness. I knew I could do some serious damage if I fell here and I would still be alone – dying.

I had one chance to hit the button. I could only heave my arms a single time. I bent over and swung upwards with both arms hoping my left arm, which was nearest the button on the wall, would stay up long enough and be high enough to make impact. The slender splints on my arms extended out over my bandaged fingers and I had to hit the button just right with the tip of the splint in order to engage the button.

As my arm came down, my splint hit something as I fell in a pile on the floor between the chair and the wall. In despair I thought I had missed the button and all had been for naught. Then I heard the clicking sound above me and a voice said, "Can I help you?"

I almost cried in pain because my limbs felt like they were about to snap off, and in relief that I had made contact. I said, "I am dying and I don't want to be alone."

The lady's voice, coming from somewhere on another floor in the hospital, told me to hold on that there would be somebody with me in a minute. She kept the line open and talked to me as she alerted somebody of the situation. I was in agony, I was dying, but at least I had a voice with me. She kept asking if I was OK.

"Yes," I said, "keep talking to me."

She asked if I was in bed and I told her I was on the floor.

I heard an alarm go off in the hallway and the loudspeaker called out that there was an emergency in room 4272. It was probably another twenty seconds or so when people burst in through the door forgetting the protocol with masks and gowns and setting the room ablaze with light.

There was a swarm of faces around me as the chair and bed were pushed away. People shouted at me and at each other all at once asking what was wrong, if I was hurt, if I was alright.

When I got the chance I said, "I am dying and I don't want to be alone." Everybody just stopped and looked at me and there was silence in the room for at least ten seconds. Then, all at once, they assessed the situation and got busy, attempting to get me up and get me to the bed. There was really no place to hold me that would make it easy, and I didn't have any strength left to help myself, so I knew this was going to hurt. They were all talking now and working with an urgency to get me back in bed. I thought they might be angry but they were not.

Two nurses folded blankets and placed them under my arms as two more untangled me from the chair, wall and floor. While they worked to get me back in the bed my adrenalin was pumping and I was hurting like you cannot imagine. But I was happy that somebody was with me and I wouldn't be alone as I died. My sense of inner alarm started to ease.

It was around 4:30 am. The voice in the wall asked if I needed more assistance. The people working with me said I was going to be alright and turned off the voice with a push of the button and I simply said, "Thanks."

As I was maneuvered into the bed and reconnected to the various wires and tubes I knew I was going to be OK. The feeling that I was going to die was gone.

I will never know if things would have been different if I had not struggled to get to the button. Maybe I needed to move to right whatever was wrong with me internally; maybe it was all in my head. Whatever the case, I felt better.

Once the nurses and attendants were sure I was alright and "no longer dying" as I termed it, things calmed down.

Then something special happened. Throughout the rest of the night and the next day I got short visits from nurses, doctors, interns, and staff – most people I didn't know nor who knew me. They brought magazines and read to me, one picking up as the other left off, showing me pictures, reading or just sitting there trying to pass the time for me. I was never awake alone after that night.

This became a ritual with staff for the next week or more. Somebody had set up an informal schedule of coffee and lunch breaks so that they could pass the time with me and I would not be by myself. Some brought treats and some brought french fries and helped me eat them. The visits continued until after I was able to sleep right through the night.

Sleeping through the night was a long time coming. My body was exhausted and traumatized and I thought it should have been easy. *Just close your eyes and let nature take its course.* However that was not to be.

Each night I tried different things until one night I realized that I had never said my nightly prayers. That was something I had done ever since I could remember. First Mom had taught us our prayers and when we were able to recite the "Angel of God" she asked us every night if we had said them and we always did. Me and Sharon would recite the prayer out loud together before going to sleep.

Tonight there would be no Sharon to add to my voice so in
my head I started the "Angel of God" as I used to do. At the end
I said, "Good night, Sharon, good night Francis, good night
Richard, good night Harold, good night Barry, I love you all and
I dearly miss you all, you will fill my dreams." I slept soundly until
the morning. First time! That was it; it was what I had been missing. I carried that tradition forward and I still say it to this day.

*"The turning point in the process of growing up is when you
discover the core of strength within you that survives all hurt."*
~ Max Lerner, *The Unfinished Country*, 1950

I began having more visitors during the days. It was difficult
for my family to come visit from North Harbour but they took advantage of any opportunity. Mary was already in St. John's so she
came every evening after work. She lived with a couple of other
girls her age and although she didn't have a car she would take
the bus or somebody would drop her off.

My tubes and wires had all been removed two days after I had
my "dying" night. My leg was sealed so water couldn't get on the
bandage and I was returned to having daily baths to remove skin
from other burned areas of my body.

It was easy to have others attend to me but if I wanted to get
out of here I had to do for myself. When the nurses came in the
next morning to wheel me for my bath, I asked if I could walk out.
They looked at each other and said, "Why not?" At least I could
give it a try. Since I was on the ward alone and there was no way
in except through the double doors by my room where visitors
could ring the bell, the nurses decided there was no need to cover
me up. To drape a sheet over me would have been difficult anyway
so three nurses planned to form a "bumper pad" squad while one
came behind with the wheelchair.

First I had to be readied; all the bandages had to be removed (and each day less and less of the bandages were sticking). So with a little help I got out of the bed and stood by myself on the floor in my bare feet, naked to the world with the exception of the few bandages.

The tiled floor felt cool and refreshing as I stood there waiting to move. As the nurses positioned themselves around me I tentatively made my way to the bathtub across the hall. It took about ten minutes to make the trek but it was a revitalizing ten minutes. I swayed and wobbled my way to the tub and the nurses helped me get in. As I sank into the warm yellow water I felt like I had just climbed a mountain. The trip back was in a wheelchair.

Over the next couple of days I got much stronger and the trip to the bathtub became almost a normal walk, but because my feet were wet and my wounds more open from the water, I always had to return in the wheelchair. Still, I bragged to Mary and whoever else came to see me about being up walking again.

Every day there were piles of cards and best wishes coming in. There were teddy bears everywhere along the window and on the night table, and on downturned boxes that were makeshift shelves on the floor.

It was like a ritual when the mail came. One of the nurses would read all the cards and I would pick where they would be attached to the wall. Visitors seemed to know there were lots of teddy bears, however they continued to bring them on "first visits."

Neil came; he had hitchhiked from North Harbour to spend a few hours with me. I was so happy to see him as I had not seen him since the hospital in Placentia. I was so glad that he was OK. He told me that Eddy was going to Calgary for work. I was sad about that.

As hard as it was for me in the hospital, I didn't have to live with the daily reminder of a blackened ground and a huge fresh clay-covered hole in the graveyard. So much had changed for my brothers and they were only young men. One day they lived at home with a huge family; the next day it was all gone. Eddy had lost his best friend in Francis, Neil had lost his best friend in Richard, and Larry had just had his eighteenth birthday and should be looking forward to a rewarding future.

When Neil left that day I had no idea when I would see him again, but I had enjoyed getting some news from home. However, my family was shrinking by degrees. Now they had no home, half their family was gone and the easiest way for Eddy to deal with it, I guessed, was to make a complete change that he could control.

Before the end of June I had a postcard from Calgary addressed to me at the hospital – it was from Eddy and simply said, "Get Well Soon." He was thinking about me when he got there.

When Mom had gone home after her first visit to the hospital and told Dad how terrible I looked and that she thought I would die, Dad told the boys that I would not be the same ever again, and that I would look different. Neil didn't know what to expect and Eddy didn't want to know because he was already having such a hard time dealing with the loss. He was there when the bodies were retrieved and thought I must look the same.

When my aunt Marg came to see me for the first time, I recognized her immediately beneath all the green clothing. She stepped into the room and said hello and asked how I was but never looked at me where I was propped up in the bed. She went to the wall and looked at all the cards and read every one of them out loud. She added hers to the collection.

Then she looked at all the teddy bears and back to the cards again. I said, "Marg, please turn and look at me," and she did, slowly. As her eyes met mine I could see the tears and she started to bawl. I told her I was alright which helped break the ice and then it was as if I hadn't left home at all. We struck up a conversation until it was time for her to go, and she shed another few tears before leaving.

Marg was married to my mom's brother Dick and I was so happy that she had come to see me. I knew she would have been a person who my mother leaned on. It was important for her to know that I was doing well.

My aunt May – my mother's sister – and her husband Cecil came to see me quite often from St. Mary's. May kept telling me to get better because my mother needed me so much. I knew she was right and I was trying so hard. She told me she was happy to see me improving and that meant a lot to me.

One day there was a bit of excitement on the ward; a new patient was coming in. There was an older gentleman from some part of western Newfoundland who had had his chest and arm burned and he wasn't responding to treatment at one of the western hospitals. He was being brought in by ambulance. This I heard by way of my partially closed door. He was in his seventies and would be here for a week or so. Bonus, I thought. I wouldn't be by myself in this part of the hospital.

Sure enough Mr. C. arrived and was placed in the room next to mine. Although we couldn't see each other, he knew I was in the next room and gestured my way each day. Mr. C. couldn't talk but he wrote a few things on paper or made gestures and noises to communicate. Since his burns were more progressively healed than mine, he had fewer restrictions on visitors then I did, and he was allowed to leave his room although he wasn't allowed to come in mine. But because he came from far away he did not get any visitors and so he was quite lonely.

After a few days, one of the nurses discovered he had a love of accordion music – and that it was his birthday. She managed to get an accordion and practiced playing "Happy Birthday" at home. The next day the nurses had cake and played for Mr. C. They left my door open and he came outside to blow out his candles. I sang "Happy Birthday" from my bed.

Mr. C. took the accordion and played a few tunes from his room for all the nurses, loud enough so I could hear. One of the nurses asked if it bothered me and I told her that I also loved accordion music and not to worry.

Next day my door was opened half way and Mr. C. waved at me from the opening, pulled up a chair outside and played me a few tunes on the accordion. He didn't talk, but the music was his voice to the world and what a beautiful voice it was. He continued this ritual until he left the hospital and was sent to a convalescent home in western Newfoundland.

While Mr. C. was in the room next door I still had to cross the hall to have a bath. Since I could now walk with more ease, I refused to get back in the wheel chair in order to get to the bath.

I was steadier on my legs and one nurse would walk with me while another would carry a sheet on two outstretched arms in order to conceal my movement from Mr. C. They always warned him it was my bath time and not to come out and he always complied; however they carried the sheet as a precaution.

My days followed the same pattern, bath in the morning, bandages changed then back to the bed. In the evening my bandages had to be changed again before I was settled for the night. Four times a day I got a dose of morphine, and later during the hospital stay, valium.

Dr. Anderson came and felt it was time for the bandage on my leg to go as he figured it would be healed by now. After he left, one of the nurses came in preparing to remove it. Of all the luck I could have had with nurses, this one was the least gentle. She was well meaning but somehow or other she always managed to hurt me in some way. I hoped this time would be different.

She prepared a bowl of warm water just in case but said she didn't think I would need it. She pushed the blanket back on my naked body and I could see the bandage that ran around the side of my body from just above my knee to just below my bellybutton. There were strips of tape along each edge and criss-crossed over the middle, up, down and across.

She started to pull the tape off the inside of my leg first. She took her time and with each tug on the tape I could see the skin rise and let go as she moved up my body. The pain was bad but bearable and I knew there was nothing she could do about the tape. It had to come off.

After almost a half an hour of having the tape removed she finally pulled the last piece from my belly. I didn't realize how tense I had been until the last piece of tape let go and my body relaxed. Finally I thought, it was over and hadn't been too bad.

I figured the tape was the worst of it and it was only a matter of lifting the bandage off and tossing it in the garbage. The nurse grabbed the bottom edge of the bandage above my knee and ripped the bandage off in one fluid motion.

I screamed as my body lifted off the bed in pain and I watched as what looked like pieces of flesh dropped from the edge of the bandage onto my leg. I clenched my teeth as I bit back the scream that was about to come out again. My leg and hip were on fire and stinging in pain. The nurse looked at me and then looked at my leg and said she had to go get the doctor as she rushed for the door. I think I had scared her when I screamed and my leg certainly didn't feel right and I guessed by the way her eyes bulged that it probably didn't look right either.

While she was gone my leg was exposed to the air and I could feel the coolness on the skin and it helped dull the pain that came in waves, diminishing a little at a time. In all I had gone through and I had felt since coming in to the hospital, this was one of the worst experiences.

I looked down to study the wound. The bandaged area was much larger than the actual skin graft site, which started about halfway up my thigh and ended right at the bend in my hip. I tried to bend my knee to get a better look but any movement caused the pain to become stronger.

There were squares of skin missing from my leg. Within the squares I could see other tinier squares, like a mesh covering the wound. In some places it looked like the mesh was still there while in others just the imprint remained. There were tiny square holes in the skin that must have gone with the bandage when it was torn off. Some of these tiny squares were bleeding and some were just there like sinkholes in the skin. The entire site was throbbing in pain and I continued to grit my teeth against it in hopes that it would subside. If I was able to clench my fists I would have done so but that was impossible.

An intern came in and looked at the wound and called Dr. Anderson. The intern got a sterile pack and took out a pair of tweezers. He poked around each of the squares removing any of the mesh that was remaining. The wound looked really wet and sticky when he was done. He said they would leave it open to the air for a few days to let it heal.

If I had been able to at the time I think I would have run away but unfortunately I was stuck in the bed and had to take it as it came. I was ordered an extra shot of some sort of drug and that knocked me out for a while.

When I woke the sheet was over the wound and it was still throbbing only a little less aggressively than before. The nurse came in again and lifted the sheet to see how it was doing. The sheet was wet and sticking to the area so I asked if she could just tuck it in everywhere else and leave the area open to the air. She did as I asked, I was given some more drugs and that helped ease the pain for a restless night.

The next day Rusty was back and when she came in she looked at my leg and asked what happened. I told her and I couldn't help myself as tears began to stream down my face, although I didn't sob or cry. I told her I had wished it was her that had taken off the bandage because I knew she would be gentle. I said that the other nurse usually hurt me, even though I didn't believe she meant to do it.

Rusty tended to my wound, bathing it with warm water and applying a soothing cream to help the pain go away. When she was leaving I heard her say that I wouldn't have to worry about that nurse again. I told Rusty she didn't mean to hurt me, it was just her way. But Rusty was like a momma bear with a cub. She said she didn't care, she was making sure the nurse would be scheduled somewhere else. I felt really bad and I told her so. Rusty said not to worry, that nothing would happen to the nurse, she simply would be scheduled somewhere else. I asked if she was sure because I could take it, I hadn't meant to cry. Rusty said she was sure and that I should put it out of my mind. I never did see the nurse again in the Burn Unit.

I suffered great pain for a couple of days. The drugs helped dull it but I couldn't turn my leg and I couldn't get comfortable. Despite the sheepskin padding, my heels and my elbows began to form sores from lying on my back. The nurses rolled sheets and placed them under my ankles and my arms to keep the sores from resting on the bed. This was supposed to help them heal but it was another slow and painful process.

I began physiotherapy and occupational therapy as soon as it was possible. My arms were seizing up and I was starting to hunch over as the skin tightened over my limbs. When the physiotherapist came for me I would have to do stretches and exercises to make sure I could regain muscle. Whatever the therapist gave me to do in that hour I spent with him or her, I would try to surpass. If I had to move two inches, I moved four.

In the time I spent by myself in the room I made sure I practiced and practiced. I wanted to get out of here and go back to what I knew, where I might find safety, where I might find that this wasn't real. I wanted to go home. Although I was fifteen, I was a little girl thrown into an adult situation and I was finding it difficult to adapt and to cope.

My right arm was also not doing well. It was twisting and the skin was tightening to a point that the arm was deforming. The daily physiotherapy helped but unfortunately there was only so much my body could take. The shoulder blade on the right side had moved so that my arm didn't have the mobility it required to get a full range of motion. Because of the burns there was no exercise possible that would put the shoulder blade back where it belonged and it was going to be a permanent impairment.

A metal arm splint was ordered for my right arm. Again people showed up dressed in green with trays of metal and padding to make the splint.

I lay in the bed as the metal was assessed and cut. My bandaged arm was measured several times before the green men left to heat and manipulate the metal to fit it.

When they returned, the metal pieces had been adjusted and capped so there was nothing sharp that could hurt me. They assembled them around my arm, applying sponge padding on top and on the plastic hand splints on my wrist. The device was tied firmly to my arm with stiff bandages that pulled my arm to the point where it physically would not go any straighter. It was very uncomfortable but was necessary if I wanted to regain its full use. I wore it day and night except for bath time and physio time, and bore the discomfort as I had everything else.

Every second day or so the bandage was pulled tighter and tighter and I could notice that the arm was responding positively. I was glad that something was working for me physically but mentally I was not doing so well. Although on the outside I tried to be happy and positive when people were around, on the inside I was sad and withdrawing.

I wanted and needed something to be normal.

Before Mr. C. left, the ward got busy again. Two more patients were admitted within days of each other. One was a father of two small children and the other was a man in his early thirties who came from a large family and had many brothers and sisters in and out each day. The Burn Unit was bursting at the seams.

With all the activity I was "adopted" almost immediately by both of the families. Although they couldn't come in the room, visitors for the other two patients stopped at my door and had a chat before moving on. They brought me treats and none of the family members ventured on the ward without a milkshake for me. The two patients always asked their visitors when they got there if they had been to see me. If they hadn't, they were made go back.

All this activity helped lift my spirits for a little while although it would never replace visits from my family and friends.

The wife of one of the patients stopped by and asked me lots of questions about what her husband would have to go through and how the children would adjust. I told her that her husband would be out before I would and that what she was seeing now would not be what he would be like in a week. Sure enough about a week later he was ready to be released and they were ecstatic. Before leaving they stopped by with a gold locket for me from their family and hoped I would get better soon.

I prayed their wish for me would come true.

I received cards, sometimes weekly, from people who couldn't be with me during the summer. My father's sister, my aunt Nelly, whom I had never seen, wrote me every week from Boston hoping that I was doing much better. She always asked about Dad. I had never seen this woman in my life. She had moved to Boston when she was a teenager and to my knowledge never returned. But she genuinely cared about my wellbeing.

I had notes from teachers who were gone away for the summer and in particular I had many letters from Sister Rose Crawford, my high school principal. She wrote almost weekly telling me she was thinking about me and my family and that she was praying for me every day.

The first time Sister Rose had come to see me she had gotten such a fright that she ran out of the room to get the nurse. She finally came back in when she realized that I was swelled beyond recognition but that it was indeed me. I was knocked out on drugs and never knew she was there so I did not know the impact I had had on her in those first few minutes.

Gerard came by often and he would speak to the nurses and the doctors and relayed messages to my mother and father on how I was doing. And, of course, Mary would visit every day that she could. If she wasn't gone to North Harbour, she was at the hospital each evening after work. I looked forward to her visits and missed her when she was gone.

My mother came to see me whenever she could as well. She told me on one visit that they were going to build a new house and that Dad wanted to know where I wanted to build it. Dad said he could get land somewhere else or we could build in the same yard where the other house was. I said I couldn't imagine living anywhere else in the Harbour and if he was going to build then I was OK with building back where I knew, where I was home.

Something inside me hoped that maybe we could push a restart button and everything would be back as it was. I hadn't come to grips with the enormity of what happened, I hadn't cried, I hadn't grieved. I existed day to day, taking each as it came and dealing with whatever it held.

I talked to God when I was alone and told him that I would go through this once for my mother and father, to give them something to live for and concentrate on as they tried to cope with what they had lost. I told Him I would be strong and make my parents proud but that I would not let them know I was suffering in any way. I asked Him to help me with that. I also told Him that if there was a second time that I would simply give up. I didn't have it in me to fight the battle twice – once for sure, but twice never.

People came to visit from all over as I was getting stronger. Some of my friends from school came to see me and asked what I would like, most brought cards and flowers or teddy bears. My room was slowly filling up.

Some of the girls my age from home came to see me one day and wanted to know if they could get me anything. I jokingly said I wanted a new sports car. They left to go to the Avalon Mall a short time later and returned with a little gold Porsche Dinky and said my wish had come true.

It was so special to get to see my friends and pretend that I was alright, that things weren't crazy or haywire. I cherished their visits; it was the closest I could get to normal without being in a place where I could be normal. They treated me as they would if I were home and that felt good.

Lots of adults came as well. Some were friends of my parents or my brothers, some were teachers, and some were relatives that I only got to see a few times a year. People helped pass the time for me.

My mother's cousin, Thomas Dalton, and his wife Catherine had several daughters living in St. John's who came to see me quite a bit. The Daltons had lost their youngest child, Jackie, the year before from an illness – she was Francis' age and the Dalton girls were all friends with my older siblings.

Thomas and Catherine had been faithful weekly visitors to our house before the fire. Their house was directly across the water on the south side of North Harbour, and on almost every visit they asked Barry to sing for them. Sometimes they had Mom or Dad take Barry out of bed to sing a couple of songs for them if they arrived later than usual. Barry was so small but he was a good singer even when he was only a couple of years old and was always happy to do it. It made him feel special – and so he was. Sometimes they would give him a quarter which made him even more eager to do it. The Daltons continued to visit with my parents for many years after the fire. I guess they could connect in some way with my parents' loss.

The police also came to see me a couple of times but neither Rusty nor the doctors would let them in my room. They said I was not strong enough to be questioned. I didn't know why they needed to talk to me but many strange things were becoming my reality.

That summer was one of the best on record for temperatures, and I gazed longingly out the window on days when I was alone – staring at the street, the cars, and trying to make sense of what had happened. I often thought about the "used to be" times, and they were so good.

Our house was in the "middle" of North Harbour and if it wasn't the middle it was most definitely the center of attention almost every day. There was the "up-along" crowd – Burtons, Bonias, Olivers, and Trembletts – and there was the "down-along" crowd – the Powers, Walshs, Philpotts, Brewers and Leonards. Every day after school or during the summer the up-along crowd came down and the down-along crowd came up and our yard was the gathering spot for everyone. Since most families had eight or ten children, and there were ten of us, it didn't take long for there to be a crowd. We got to hang out and play games with the older and younger children from all over the Harbour.

For as long as I could remember there were trails in the woods behind our house where we played cops and robbers or cowboys and indians in the summer and fall. Next to these trails there was a "town" built in the woods where we joined the older ones for many games of hide-and-seek. The town was built on the hill in the woods and had streets, a jail, a hotel, a hospital, and many other features that our imagination could conjure and our hands could build from sticks and boughs. Everyone helped build an "Olympic stadium" area where we had a high jump, a long jump, and many other games that we all took turns playing. The hill behind the house or the yard was always full of children.

One summer the older boys got really creative and gathered tires that were abandoned out on the road and placed them in an "army course" to add to the other games. They built climbing walls, rope ladders and a whole series of activities that would have made the Canadian Armed Forces proud. It was a wonder nobody was hurt as they raced through the obstacle course trying to best one another. There were no medals, just the honor of saying that somebody won on a particular day. Thirty to forty kids would compete; sometimes there would be so many, the games would be separated into age groups and the older ones would keep order and scores. There were always woodpiles for climbing and playing "house" for the younger ones if the Olympics or the army course got too competitive.

After the time changed in the fall and it was dark early in the evenings our yard would fill for games of tag and spotlight. There could be forty or fifty children between eight and eighteen out playing all around our yard.

In the winter we went on Soaker's Path or down the Ridge when there was enough snow for homemade slides and toboggans. When Soaker's Path got nice and slippery it was time to bring out the big toboggan. Lloyd and Bonnie Oldes from the US Naval Base in Argentia had given Dad an old aluminum toboggan and we could sit three big kids side by side, four or five rows deep on it. If we managed to make the turn on the bottom of the hill we could go right down over our meadow to the snow buffer that was set up by the fence next to the house. Of course if we didn't make it we ended up in the woods and had to go back and start again. The older children would fix the turn on the path to resemble a bobsled run so that we always made it to the bottom.

I remembered winter days when we would be out on the road between our house and the churchyard playing ball hockey. The snow plow would have gone down and left enough snow on each side of the road to keep the ball out of the ocean or the ditch. Mom's brother-in-law, Cecil Critch, drove the snow plow and always made sure that place on the road was good for a game of hockey. Sometimes their whole family would come from St. Mary's and join in with the rest of the kids from the Harbour.

We would be on the road for hours and every now and again a group of us would go in the house and Mom or Dad would dry our wool mitts and socks over the stove, give us a cup of hot tea, and dress us up to go out again before another shift of children came in to repeat the ritual.

Our place was always the hub of activity well past dark every evening. When we were called in for the night, our friends made their way home.

My parents never cared how many were at the house. There was so much childhood innocence at that time, so much fun and togetherness. I was sure that our family weren't the only ones who would be feeling the loss. The whole community had changed and grown up that day. I dreamed of those carefree days and wished I could get them back.

Myself and Sharon were particularly close. We spent many hours in the shed playing table tennis on a makeshift table made from two small pieces of plywood and a rolled-up towel as the net. Sharon was very competitive at school because of all our practice.

We drank mugs of Tang in the shed playing on rainy days when we couldn't get outside. If we weren't playing table tennis it was playing house and dolls with our cousins and several of our friends. Our imagination knew no limits. I was going to miss her. To pass the time I relived those days over and over.

There were so many hours spent out on the hill in our back meadow playing "grounders." The older boys would take turns batting a rubber ball into a group of however many children were around to play. There were so many points for catching it in the air, so many for one bounce and so many for on the ground. We played this for hours until almost everyone had a chance to win, and wrestling matches would break out in the middle of the game if a couple of people needed an extra point or so. It was so much laughter and camaraderie.

This had to be a dream that I could wake up from sometime soon. There was no way this could be real. This didn't happen to people like us. It just didn't.

I was growing tired of being in bed, somebody feeding me, somebody reading to me, somebody bathing me, or just looking out the window to pass the time. I was longing for home.

This was the time of the year when we should have all been in on the marshes picking bakeapples. Every year since I was old enough to make the almost two-hour daily trek, I would join the rest of my family picking berries so we could sell them to get school clothes and supplies. Dad had a doctor lined up from St. John's who bought all the berries at a fair price. Every day some of us would bring the berries down to the Shop and Jose would weigh them. Dad always wanted to make sure that he wasn't "wronging" anyone.

It was fun to spend the whole week with whatever family was home. Dad would bring a tin can to use as a kettle, we would have a little campfire and some tea and toast in the woods before heading for home. My brothers would tease each other and romp around in between the berry picking and Mom or Dad would have to remind them what they were there for.

It was a long walk and everyone would be going home with buckets of berries. Dad would put ours in a knapsack that he carried until we were old enough to carry our own. He always showed us points of reference in case we ever got lost.

When September came we would go after the blueberries growing on the hill not far from the house. I remembered when myself and Sharon, Harold and Barry were younger we weren't allowed to go. We would wait in the yard until we heard the excited voices of Mom and Dad and our older siblings as they came into view at the top of the hill. They would always have a couple of blueberry bushes broken off for each of us so we could pick our own berries. I could almost smell the jam and pies cooking in the kitchen.

I was closer with Sharon, Harold and Barry than I was with any of the others simply because of our ages. We spent many hours playing inside and outdoors. Some rainy days we would stand in the doorway in the porch and see who could run to the well house on the river and back the quickest. We spent hours trying to beat each other's times. Mom would be mad at us for getting wet but we would be allowed to continue because it kept us busy and out from under foot.

In the winter Francis, Eddy, Neil and Richard would build tunnels for us out in the snow banks. Sometimes the snow was so high they had to put a ladder at the back of the tunnel so we could climb out.

Everyone was happy, that was the only way to describe it. Times were simple but they were good. We were poor but we had lots. There was always a smell of something baking in the house.

Every year Dad put up a set of swings made from sticks in the woodpile and ropes from the stable. There were always five or six swings going at the same time. He always had a horseshoe pit somewhere in the yard and spent hours with the older boys pitching the shoes.

I remembered one time in particular when Dad and Richard were playing and I happened to be swinging near the horseshoe pit. Richard threw the shoe and it slipped out of his hand and got caught in the rope on my swing. I looked up as it was coming down and ended up with seven stitches in my forehead. He felt so bad but I was fine and was treated to an ice cream in Placentia. After seeing the doctor that was a real treat. I tried to reach for the scar as the memory passed through my mind, but unfortunately I could not touch it.

Dad always made soccer nets in the yard in the summer and the place would fill with kids. Sometimes Mom would come out and join the fun. There was no sitting out or no positions, just everyone out running around and having a great time.

We also had a TV, which was a novelty at best for most of the kids in the Harbour. On rainy days Dad would joke that there was no place to lay a foot down in the living room with everyone on the floor, hands under jaw, watching TV.

I guess that happy life contributed to the "good naturedness" of all of us.

Francis was the life of any party. If there was a party anywhere in St. Mary's Bay, I am sure he would be invited. He would leave with his guitar and play and sing all night long. I smiled as I thought of the time, before going to college to earn a civil engineering diploma, he decided to leave for the mainland. He made it as far as the CN ferry at Port aux Basques and played his guitar going across on the boat, and when he got to the other side he decided to come back and repeated the performance. He was gone a week at the most. Mom and Dad were so sad when he went and so happy when he returned.

When he finished his diploma program, Francis went to work as a civil engineer with the provincial Department of Transportation. Eddy was working as an electrician and between them both they would buy things for Mom and Dad, such as a new chesterfield set, washer and dryer or chainsaw. They also brought toys for us younger kids.

When Richard started working as an appraiser and Neil at electrical, they also helped pay for things for Mom and Dad. My brothers would pick out something that our parents needed and they would all pitch in. They were very good to our parents and we all expected that we would follow in their footsteps.

Richard loved to hang out with the crowd as well but he had no talent for singing. He was always in a good mood and was just a nice person to be around, always joking and having fun. He made friends very easily and didn't mind helping anybody out.

Mom often spoke about the year that he really needed a pair of boots. He was in college and had no money to get anything for himself. Both he and Neil would hitchhike back and forth to St. John's on Fridays and Sundays to go to college. Mom couldn't bear to have him cold because he had nothing to put on his feet except an old pair of sneakers lined with cardboard soles. The weather turned cold early that year and she got some money from Nanny Power and bought a pair of boots, giving them to him in November. He called her his "angel of mercy" for fitting him out with the boots which would have been his Christmas present.

None of us ever took anything for granted and were always grateful for everything our parents were able to give us, the older ones especially because they had seen the poorest times out of us all.

My thoughts were interrupted as Dr. Anderson strolled in. Back to reality!

There were two huge bulging red scars forming at the base of my neck. As they were growing and spreading the fear was that they might restrict airflow in my throat. Because it was in an area that was delicate and hard to operate on, Dr. Anderson decided he would try a new procedure first to see if he could minimize the scars.

He explained to me that the plan was to air-force medication into the scars using an instrument that was similar to a small gun. He said it might hurt and for me to prepare myself.

I watched as the liquid was loaded into this shiny gun and noticed that the barrel that would be placed against my neck was a little bit bigger than a dime and was full of pinholes. The doctor explained that the gun would rapidly force the medication through the holes, puncturing the outer layer of the scar and hopefully shrinking it over time.

I believed it was going to hurt but not much didn't hurt anymore; I was prepared to take it. However, I should have known that it was going to be so much more than that. Dr. Anderson was on one side of the bed and there was a nurse on the right side of me holding my shoulder down and a nurse next to the doctor holding my other shoulder down.

He asked, "Ready?" and I said, "Yes!" I heard the click of the gun immediately as pain blasted through my throat. Tiny spatters of blood passed through my vision as well as white little stars. Before I could make a sound, I heard the click again, felt the pressure of the nurses holding me down, and tears automatically spilled from my eyes. Click number three, and that one was over.

The skin at the base of my throat was on fire. I couldn't speak because I thought I would cry. My eyes were as big as saucers as I looked at Dr. Anderson and he kept repeating, "I am so sorry, I am so sorry, but this has to be done."

When I got my voice back I asked if that was it and he said, "No, it's the first one. I still have to do the other."

I asked if I could have a minute and he said yes, but just a minute because he wanted to get it done. I nodded that I was ready and he wiped some alcohol over the first scar and then the next one in preparation for the treatment to resume.

This time I knew what I was dealing with so I tried to think of happy thoughts. There were none. I lay there and felt the nudge on my skin where the gun was resting and then I heard the click. My eyes watered again, the pain was unbearable and then there were three more clicks and it was over.

The nurses got me some water and a Popsicle and pressed some cold cloths on the area that had been treated. On a pain scale of one to ten, this was a twenty. I still couldn't speak as the waves of pain ebbed and flowed and gradually decreased. Dr. Anderson asked if I was alright and I nodded. He waited with his hand resting on my shoulder and I could see in his eyes that he had hated the pain he had caused.

When I could speak I told him I was OK and he said he hoped

this would work and that he wouldn't have to do it twice. I said, "It better because I can't do this again."

He stayed for another little while as the ice-cold cloth helped ease the pain. When my eyes began to dry, he patted my head and told me I was his star patient. Then he turned and was gone.

For the next two days the base of my throat could not be soothed. It stung and stung and I had to be medicated to ease the pain. A couple of extra needles in the leg and many cold cloths later the pain died away. Dr. Anderson told me it was looking great. The treatment worked. I was so relieved because I would have done it again if it was required. I always did as I was told.

I was physically and mentally drained and it was very hard to stay strong and positive. The doctors and nurses, and my family were very worried that I was not showing any emotion about the whole ordeal. It was still unreal to me and I was hoping I would go home and it would be a dream.

With the exception of Mary, who visited mostly every evening, I saw none of my family very often. Mom and Dad were busy building a new house so I would have something to go home to.

It was like the universe had turned upside down. I used to only see Mary on weekends and the rest of my family all the time. Now I saw Mary every day and Mom on a rare occasion when she could visit, and none of my family could get in to see me.

I got lots of cards and letters and was excited when the mail came or when there was a commotion in the hall because that meant there might be a visitor. Many people from North Harbour called almost every day and the nurses would relay messages. The Ladies Auxiliary at the Health Sciences Centre paid for a TV for me, which was something to distract me during the day. Mary brought me homemade fries and gravy every evening, no matter what. That was her way of trying to ease the situation and bring a little bit of "home" to my room.

Every time I had the french fries I thought of the days we would all run off the bus knowing that we would have fries that day. There were nine of us on the bus at one point, but had dwindled to five this past year. The first person off the bus would shout, "First lot!" the second would shout, "Second lot!" and so on. I always liked to wait until last because then mine would be fresh. Homemade fries brought home so close.

"The soul would have no rainbow had the eyes no tears."
~ John Vance Cheney

One day in early August a card came in a red envelope. It had a Boston postmark on it and my cousin Gerard brought it in with him when he came to visit, with another few pieces of mail. Gerard opened the envelopes and read the cards to me before posting them on the wall.

When he opened the red envelope there was a beautiful white card with a red rose on it. Appropriately, it was a note from Sister Rose. Gerard started to read:

My dear Ida,

It is a few days since my arrival in Boston and I now realize I'm a week late in getting this off to you. You've been on my mind every day and I remember you and your family daily in my thoughts and prayers. I remember you all particularly at daily mass!

There were a number of things I wanted to say to you during my visits to your room but you were never alone and I didn't like to monopolize the time others had with you. Ida, I know you must have physical pain! You have been optimally courageous in bearing it, but sometimes when you have the opportunity, share that with others. They won't be able to help much but just your talking about it may help you.

Also I'm sure you often think of Sharon and your deceased brothers...

That was it, the floodgates opened and I started to wail – it was a heartbroken cry of anguish, loss, frustration, loneliness and pity all rolled up into one and I drew myself into as much of a fetal position as I could muster. I couldn't be consoled and I couldn't control it.

Gerard got the nurse but there was nothing either one of them could do. I sobbed and screeched until my stomach hurt. I made the sounds of a wounded animal and that is, in fact, what I felt like. Gerard and the nurse left the room and closed the door so that I could be alone.

I cried and cried, not knowing why, but it released a combination of sadness, pain, and loss all rolled up into one package of devastation – and devastation wasn't even strong enough to describe it. After what must have been an hour, I was exhausted and spent.

Gerard came back in and quietly sat while I lay in silence. The only sound was my uncontrollable hiccup-sighs every few minutes.

When I got myself under control I asked Gerard to finish the card and he started it again from the beginning and finished it. When he had the rest of the mail opened and read he sat again for a little while and told me how glad he was to see me cry. He said it was part of the healing process and that they were all very worried because I was so calm and collected.

We talked for a little while and I pondered on what he said. After Gerard left, I thought about what had happened and decided that I couldn't pity myself or else I would never get out of here. I was prepared to work harder than ever to make that happen.

I thought about what Sister Rose wrote long into the night. I never did talk about anything, none of us did.

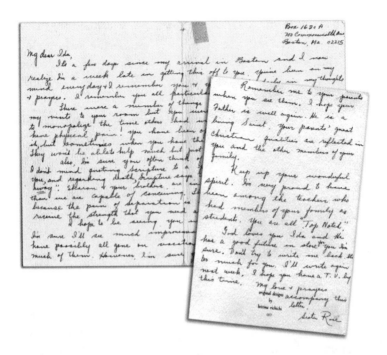

A few days later Dr. Anderson said I needed another surgery to loosen some of the scars to give me more mobility. This time when I went to the OR they wanted to give me the same paralyzing medication I had before and I told them I wanted to be put to sleep. Dr. Anderson agreed, based on what had happened in the first surgery, and he didn't want me to stress out over it. And so it was.

I watched with apprehension as the mask was lowered over my face and heard the doctor counting backwards from ten. I heard number eight before waking up hours later back in the Burn Unit. This time I was bandaged again and my left thigh had the same hard lump stretching over it letting me know it was the donor site. My throat was sore; I didn't like that.

To distract myself from the pain, my mind drifted to home where I could pick happiness from my memories. It helped.

In the summer it was not unusual for myself, Sharon, Harold and Barry to be out around the yard after breakfast while Mom did the laundry or cleaned up. We passed away the time making "devil darn needles" to keep the little black flies away. We made them by taking pieces of Mom's yarn or some white line that came on brown paper packages of meat from the store and tying them to long finger-like rocks from the lane so that a tail would fly from them as we tossed the rocks in the air. We would do that for hours thinking that the devil darn needles really protected us from the flies, not realizing the heat of the sun had taken them away. Sometimes Larry, Neil or Richard joined us in the carefree playtime.

I could see Harold's and Barry's freckled faces and flaming red hair glistening in the sun as we laughed and played and dodged the rocks as they almost came down upon our heads. Barry was very outgoing but Harold was pretty shy everywhere except home. If I really concentrated I could almost feel the warmth of the sun on my face and the sounds of their laughter.

If Sharon was here she would laugh at me. We were such good friends: we were inseparable. God how I missed her. I could almost smell the raisin tea buns or, if Mom had extra time, a cherry cake without the cherries (as funny as that sounds) when we were planning a picnic. We would take a package of green *Freshie* mixed in a mason jar and whatever Mom had baked before going up on the hill in the meadow and settling down in the long hay in our own little world talking for hours about our dreams and what we wanted to be when we grew up. Here it was, I was almost grown up and she would never be.

Thinking of Mom cleaning up reminded me of days that she waxed the floor. They were the best! Whoever was in the house waited patiently while the smell of wax filled our nostrils until she announced the floor was dry. We put on wool socks and hit the floor like a hockey team hitting the ice and started skating around. At first the floor seemed to push back as our feet buffed and polished, but as the shine slowly emerged from the dull waxed surface the fun really started. We twirled and raced all over the room, bumping and laughing until finally Mom stepped in because it was getting "dangerous" she would scold, and because she needed to do the corners. Some of the older ones helped her with that as we settled down from all the play.

Although there was lots of fun outside, rainy days were also enjoyable. Card games or board games like Life or Payday occupied us for hours and were kept and played for years. We all sat around our huge dining room table and laughed and joked about whatever we were playing. The older boys were very patient and helpful teaching us how to play. If Dad was home he kept his eye on things because he would never stand for cheating and he preached fairness to us all whenever he had the opportunity. He wanted to instill in us the values that he held dear to his heart.

I had a distinct memory of being about six or seven years old and Richard helping us cut the bumble bees from the Sunny Bee bread plastic wrap so the younger ones could stick the bees on the windows or the walls. Mom made bread everyday but with so many to feed we sometimes supplemented with store bought bread as a treat. It didn't take much to keep us quiet and occupied and Mom never cared about smudges and fingerprints. It was part of our growing up.

The dining room table or the living room floor became a hockey rink with a balled-up wool sock as the puck when a ball wasn't available. Competition was intense when Richard and Neil took on Eddy and Francis in a friendly game. Sometimes myself and Sharon, or Harold and Barry, were asked to play but we enjoyed watching and cheering as much as joining in.

Larry never usually played because as soon as he joined in it would all go wrong. Larry was so kind and gentle once a person got to know him and he was so good to the older people in North Harbour, but he just didn't play well with us for some reason. I missed listening to him singing himself (and all of us) to sleep every night from his bed. I wondered if he still did that and where he was sleeping now.

Life sure was simple within the happy chaos: we played, we laughed, we sang, we got along. We didn't know any other way of being a family and we didn't want to know.

Thinking about home was comforting in some ways as I remembered happy times, but overwhelming to know that those times were gone. Sometimes, as I tried to figure out what was happening, I wondered if they had ever really existed. Sometimes I thought if I picked apart what was happening I could prove that it wasn't true or never happened. That would have been great.

Several days later I noticed that the dosage of the morphine was not as strong as usual. I asked what was happening and Rusty told me that I was going to be weaned off the drugs. When Dr. Anderson came in I asked him about the dosage. He verified what Rusty had said.

I boldly stated that I thought we had an agreement. He would tell me everything without question. That I would know of any changes that were required. He just looked at me and smiled and said, yes, and that he recalled that he was supposed to run things by me.

I asked if he could continue with the same amount of morphine for that day to give me time to prepare my mind and then by tomorrow I would want none.

He laughed and said there was an addictive property in the drugs and that I couldn't do it just like that. He snapped his fingers

IDA LINEHAN YOUNG

to reiterate the point. He said I had a lot of drugs in my system over the last number of months and that withdrawing from them was a process.

I stated that if he gave me the regular dose that day I would not want it tomorrow. I would be ready for the withdrawal the next day.

He said, "Very good," and nodded to Rusty who disappeared and was back with a needle that she promptly stuck in my leg. He told me again that the next day he was going to reduce the dose.

I said, "A deal is a deal and tomorrow I don't want any. Even if it is on the chart does that mean that I have to take it?"

He said that I didn't have to, but to judge that tomorrow. I knew he was skeptical but I would show him.

Next morning the nurse came in with my needle and I told her I didn't want it. She said, OK, but that it would be there if I changed my mind. I didn't.

Dr. Anderson came in when I was getting ready for the bath and he smiled and commented on my not taking the morphine. I said I pretended that I took it and that was good enough for me.

He looked astonished and said, "Really?"

"Really," I replied.

He shook his head in disbelief. He told me that it was still ordered if I changed my mind, and I said I wouldn't.

Sure enough, I went cold turkey. I never asked for the drugs. No pain was unbearable – sometimes it made me feel alive. I could do without.

As I got stronger it was time for me to start feeding myself. My arms were very tight and it was difficult to move them and my hands would not close. The occupational therapist was called to help out with some ideas.

She came up with a contraption where a fork was attached to a long stick, which would serve as a handle. Since my hand wouldn't close around the stick, a layer of sponge was taped around

114

the base, which was now almost the size of a can of soup. I could clasp that and with a bit of practice I was able to pick up some food from a plate and get my arm to move enough to get the food to my mouth. It was painful and difficult but I was able to do it and I got better every day. I wasn't allowed to use a spoon in case I tried hot liquid and scalded myself. I was proud that I could do a little bit more and more for myself and I noticed that it was because I wanted to, not because I was forced to.

As per usual Dr. Anderson came to visit me while I was in the tub. I could hear him asking Rusty what she thought – should he allow me or not? I looked at him suspiciously and asked what he was thinking of allowing me to do. He said there were no really "open wounds" on me that would prevent me from being allowed out of my room. My leg was still bandaged but sealed. I almost sat upright in the tub with the excitement.

"Hold on," he said, "I don't mean that you can go traipsing all over the hospital; I mean just that you can leave your room and sit in the waiting area with visitors if you want."

"Really?"

"Really!"

Then he said, "Only if you are good!" He laughed then because he always said I was good and his best patient. He probably said that to others but to me he sounded like he meant it and that was good enough.

Rusty smiled and said, "That also means that visitors don't have to dress up when they come to see you, but you have to wear a gown and mask if you leave the room."

I was so excited.

She also told me that my mother had phoned and said she was coming out today and had asked what would be a good time. Rusty said she should be here in about an hour.

I told Dr. Anderson to leave, he had said enough, and then I told Rusty I was turning into a prune, to get me out of the water.

They both laughed and were very happy that I was taking this new step. Dr. Anderson cautioned me to take it easy as I was only used to the small walk between the bed and the bathtub.

I told him I would and I was so excited that Mom would see that I was getting better. I was wheeled back to the bed where my arms were dressed with bandages. The hand splints were no longer required. Rusty got a pair of pants and a gown off the rack and put them on me, being careful with the arms and especially the metal splint on my right arm. I was so skinny that she picked the smallest clothes and still had to tie a good knot to keep them on me. She got me a pair of slippers that one of my visitors had brought and I was ready. Then I waited.

A knock came on the double doors as was customary because not many rang the buzzer when they were visiting. I asked Rusty if it could be Mom coming early and Rusty told me to wait to make sure it was her.

She was back in less than a minute and told me that Jose and Seb were out there. She told them to wait in the lounge on the other side of the double doors but had said nothing more. That was normal as well when people came if I was in the middle of something with the doctors or nurses.

She got a mask and put it on me and walked with me out to the lounge. As the double doors opened I felt a freedom that I could only liken to somebody who was getting out of prison after a lengthy and undeserved sentence. It was a milestone in my recovery and gave me hope. My spirits lifted as I crossed the threshold out of the Burn Unit.

Jose and Seb stood up as the doors opened and they saw me coming out with Rusty by my side. Jose cried. As I walked toward them, I said that I was expecting Mom and they confirmed she was coming today as well and should be there any minute. She had stopped at the mall to get me a few things to wear. I asked if they minded waiting for her with me in the lounge.

They both helped me to the couch as Rusty went back to the Burn Unit.

I talked with them both for a few minutes and then I heard the elevator door open. Although it had opened and closed many times since I sat down, there was something about this time that made me notice. I was sitting with my back to her, but something told me it was my mom.

When she saw Jose and Seb she rushed towards them saying, "What's wrong now, why can't you see her?" She was upset because she thought I was having something else "done" and she never liked that. I turned around as quickly as my body would allow and Jose helped me stand up. Mom realized it was me and she started to cry. She kept saying, "You're out, you're out."

I said, "Yes, I'm out!" I told her what the doctor had said and she was so happy. I stayed in the lounge and visited with the three of them until I was too tired to stay there any longer. It was so nice to be out but I didn't want to overdo it as the doctor had warned.

Jose and Seb left and Mom helped me back to the room. She gave me some underwear and socks and some loose pants and shirts that she had just purchased.

I realized that, except for the slippers, I had nothing to call my own. I really had nothing.

My lunch had arrived and the lady with the tray came to the door to tell me it was there. I told her she could come in today, that there was no need for gowns and gear. She was so happy for me and brought the tray in to my table. When she was gone, Mom took the cover off the plate and picked up the fork to help feed me. I said, "Mom, there is no need." I asked her to open the top drawer in my night stand and get me the fork. She looked at the contraption and then at me and I laughed.

She handed me the fork, which I took in my left hand, and I sat down and started to feed myself. It was awkward and difficult but I was getting better at it. Although the hand splints were gone, the metal splint on my right arm kept me from using that one and I was right-handed as well which made it even more awkward.

Mom was so excited that I could do this much. She helped me with the soup. When she left later that day her expression was relaxed and she almost looked happy. The day had been good for me but it had had a bigger impact on her. I was glad.

When Rusty came on shift the next day I asked her to help me write a letter to my parents. She got me a pen and a couple of pieces of paper and gently placed the pen between the tip of my thumb and finger. Although I made big loops for letters I was able to convey a few sentences on the paper saying I was doing well.

Rusty put it in an envelope and mailed it for me. Mom was so excited when she got the letter a few days later that she took it everywhere with her and showed it to anyone who would look. It was a good sign and hope for her that I would soon be better.

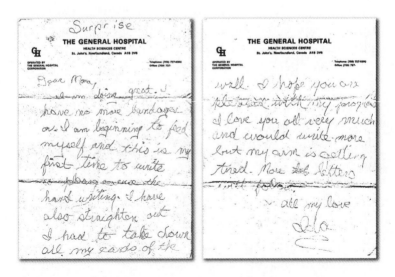

Part 2 – Going Home!

"Where we love is home – home that our feet may leave,
but not our hearts."
~ Oliver Wendall Holmes Sr.

As we travelled the dirt road towards North Harbour, I couldn't believe it – I was going home. The long arduous time at the hospital was behind me – partly. I was released as an out-patient on Friday, August 22, 1980, meaning that I had to return to the hospital from Monday to Friday every week for Sofra-Tulle dressings and physiotherapy. The best news was it also meant that I could go home on the weekends. Although I was becoming more and more resolved to the fact that there was no such place any more – at least not like I had known.

My cousin Yvonne Critch and her husband Jeff Steiner had graciously offered to bring me out to my grandparents' house in North Harbour where my mom and dad temporarily lived as they were building a new house for us. When Dr. Anderson came into the room and told me to "get out" of the hospital I was so happy and excited. He grinned as he said that I didn't have to stay there any longer. Almost ten weeks was enough for him.

I said to him, "I told you I would cut my time in half!"

He smiled widely as he said, "That you did, my child, that you did!"

When the doctor left the room after filling out all the paper work and giving me instructions for the next several months of daily visits to the hospital, I was so thrilled that I lay back across the bed and kicked up my legs with excitement. I couldn't throw my arms in the air so my legs had to do. As my legs were in mid-air on the way up for the second time, Dr. Anderson came back in through the door and laughed as he saw my celebration.

"Don't hurt yourself now!"

"I won't!"

He told me I was a pleasure to have as a patient and that he was happy it had been him who got the call the morning I came in. "Me too," I said and truly meant it, because I had had the dis-pleasure of meeting the alternative when Dr. Anderson was on vacation for two weeks during my stay.

The other doctor had come in while I was in the bathtub early on one Monday morning and grabbed me by the hair on my head (what little he could get a grip on), and pulled my head from side to side like a rag doll as I lay there soaking the bandages off my wounds. He got up and said, "Nothing wrong with you," and left the tub room within a minute of having come in.

Rusty was so mad that she whipped off her green gown as she left behind him and began telling him what she thought of his bedside manner. As the door closed in the room I could hear their raised voices in the hall. When she came back, I could see that her eyes were ready to spill with tears but she was too professional to do that. I loved Rusty so much even though I only knew her a short while. She said, "Don't you worry my baby, he will never do that with you again as long as I am a nurse!"

She was so mad and tried to cover it with a smile beneath the mask, but the smile didn't reach her eyes. I told her I was fine and that he hadn't hurt me, and really he had not because I was so used to people picking and prodding at me that I just went with whatever they were doing. I learned it was easier to do that. The next few visits from the doctor were also short but never sweet. I was so grateful when Dr. Anderson came back because I didn't have to see that ogre any more.

Now that was all behind me and I was going home! How much of my "old normal" would be there I had no way of knowing but I was desperate to find it just the same.

The long weeks in the hospital had been lonesome and hard. Every day was a struggle of some kind: pain, exhaustion and force of will to try and get better. I made it, I was going to live but what that life would be like, I had yet to find out.

Now here I was on Fairy Path Hill, twenty minutes from the world I had left almost three months before. It was getting late in the day and the sun was shining directly in our eyes. I looked behind to make sure we were still on the dirt road and could see the plumes of dust rising up from the tires and disappearing somewhere behind us. When I looked forward again I felt like I was going into the light; there was nothing but brightness and the dark outlines of Jeff and Yvonne in the front seat.

I started to rock back and forth to ease the discomfort in my limbs as I sat on the edge of the seat – ironically, not unlike the day I left. I was also getting anxious about what I was about to see.

By the time we got to North Harbour it was kind of eerie and the sun was shining on the right side of us hiding everything in dark shadows. The ocean on the left held the light and reflected the darkness in towards shore. I couldn't distinguish anything and I didn't really want to. I stared straight ahead on the way to my grandparents' house as we passed where our house used to be, and the graveyard. I had an urge to turn and look but I willed myself not to do it, and I didn't.

I looked to my right towards the Shop as we passed and it was busy as usual. I didn't know at the time but I was the topic of conversation since my mother received the news – everyone in North Harbour knew I was on my way home. The whole Harbour was excited for me and couldn't wait to see me.

As we pulled into the gravel lane in front of my grandparents' old two-storey house my mom and dad, and my grandmother and grandfather, were already in the pathway, having seen the car come over the top of Chapel Hill. There were hugs and sobs and everyone gathered around me and I forced myself once again to be strong. No tears, no tears! I bit my tongue and smiled as the urge to bawl was so strong. I was grabbed and embraced by everyone there. It hurt physically but I welcomed the pain because it took my mind off how I was hurting emotionally on the inside. I had been homesick for so long and thought I would never get back again. Over the chattering, as we made our way up the lane, I assured everyone I was great and couldn't wait to have some homemade bread and beef stew that I knew was simmering inside the small house on the old stove.

I had been in my grandparents' house many times since I was a little girl but had never been upstairs. It was just something we didn't do so it was very foreign to me to be led up the stairs and shown where I would be sleeping. Jeff dropped off the few items I had in my bag and the many cards and teddy bears that had followed me home. The hospital had packed a few sets of sterile white sheets that had to be put on my bed and brought back to the hospital with me. My mother began making the bed as I quickly unpacked my meager possessions.

At supper everyone was touching me and watching me eat. It wasn't an uncomfortable feeling – because with the exception of my mother, none of them had seen me since the day the house burned down. They were taking in the sight of me as if I were the Crown Jewels. The phone was ringing and ringing as people called to see if I made it.

I was still covered in bandages but there were a lot of healed scars to be seen. I told them not to be afraid to touch me, I didn't mind. Although it was August, the fire was lit in the old-fashioned stove in the kitchen and the place was really small. I wasn't accustomed to the heat anymore and it was overwhelming, especially after having the hot stew. I thanked Yvonne and Jeff for bringing me home and since it was so hot in the kitchen I asked if they could bring me up to the Shop on their way back to St. John's. I wanted to get that first time over with too.

The Shop was the hub of North Harbour. I had gone there almost every day in my "old life" and deep down I wanted to get to something or some place that was a "before normal." The Shop was always a typical gathering place and I enjoyed the busy-ness there. My mother came with me. She was so happy to have me home she didn't want to let me out of her sight.

I had no idea how hard it was for her or my dad. They had gone to bed one night with ten kids, nine in the house, and today, less than three months later, there was only a couple of us left. I had just arrived. Neil was working in St. John's by now, getting a ride in and out every day.

In mid August, Larry wrote supplementary exams in lieu of not having written the originals with his class, which he was supposed to do the day of the fire. News of the fire had spread to the high school that morning before the grade 11 exams began. When the North Harbour bus arrived Larry wasn't on it and the students were very upset because they thought that their classmate had died.

My cousin arrived for a scholarship exam on the same bus and he didn't really know who had made it and who had not but he was able to confirm that there were a number who died although he wasn't sure about Larry. He was in a state of shock for the most part because he had been at the scene with his father and brothers trying to help once the alarm was raised just a few hours before. The students wrote their exams and my cousin simply put "fire"on his as an answer to the questions put before him.

Larry passed his supplementary exams and was going on to college in Placentia to be a carpenter in the next couple of weeks.

Going up the steps to the Shop was difficult. I had had no exercise to speak of for the last three months and had been near death for about half of it. I had to build my strength and had to realize that I couldn't do today what I could have done back in June. That was hard for me as well. I had been so active – always running somewhere, playing some sport with all the gang, and just being outside – now I wasn't that person anymore.

The Shop was packed when I got inside and again everyone was hugging – rather lightly – and I noticed a few tears as they welcomed me home. That hurt like crazy too, but I endured it without crying because I knew everyone was so happy to see me and I was so happy to be there.

Once all the first tentative hugs were over I noticed that people were trying not to stare. I had on an oversized long-sleeved shirt so nobody could really see what was beneath. I made up my mind right then and there that I didn't want this attention, I didn't want people to be afraid of me or what I looked like. I was going to put it all out there to make them comfortable around me.

I asked Jose if I could borrow one of her daughter's halter tops. She agreed and I followed her into the house, which was attached to the Shop, and put it on. I came back out into the crowd with all my scars and bandages showing on my too-thin body. I was pretty small when I went into the hospital and came out almost twenty pounds lighter. At 5 foot 8, I was now around seventy-five pounds. The white of the bandages was stark against the red and purple marks that were visible on my bony arms, chest and back.

Everything got silent for a minute and I said, "I don't want anyone uncomfortable around me, I don't want anyone wondering what I look like or what happened to me, so please come have a look and touch me – I really want you to."

Jose was the first and she laid her hand on a part of my arm that was visible between the bandages. Tears welled in her eyes as she touched the hard smooth surface of my shoulder. The puckered skin and huge bumps were a glaring reminder of what I had gone through. Gradually everyone started talking again and people came to touch me; some people only looked because they were afraid they would hurt me and that was fine too.

As more and more people heard that I was at the Shop, more and more came and went over the next hour or so. I didn't feel uncomfortable at all, I felt strong and alive. All these people were my neighbours and my community; they were my support, and my family's support. It wasn't intrusive in any way and I wanted to get it out in the open to avoid any future awkwardness. It actually felt good that I could relax some of the bonds that I felt were tightening on me over the last few months. I was desperate to find a piece of normal. If this is was it took then this is what it took!

I was rapidly tiring and went back in to the house to get a drink of water. I asked Jose if she could pass me a glass. I told her I couldn't lift my arms too high because the skin was so tight. She got the glass and as I went to the tap she tried to get ahead of me. It was very difficult to move my hands and the palms of them were very sensitive, however I said, "Jose, thanks for wanting to help but I have to do things on my own, it's the only way I am going to get better. I will someday be able to get a glass from the cupboard even though I can't today."

She understood and said she was proud of me for taking that stand. I never did ask anyone to do anything for me that I knew deep down I was capable of doing myself. I had no trouble asking for help when I knew I couldn't do something and people were eager to help. I didn't want to get into a self-pitying state that would keep me from getting better and I was determined to get better.

After things calmed down at the Shop, we got a ride back down the road to get settled for the night. It was after nine and I was so tired, it had been a long day. But the next one would be longer.

The next morning I awoke slowly, trying to figure out where I was. I had to be careful in the morning because a sudden movement was excruciating and felt like I was ripping my skin apart. I had learned to move cautiously so my body could adjust after the night of resting in one position.

I looked around me and realized that I wasn't in the hospital bed and thought for a fleeting moment that the dream was over. Then I realized that this one wasn't my own bed either; I was not in my own house and it started to sink in that I never would be again. I still would not cry. I had to be strong for everyone around me so that this new life would not be so hard on them.

Dad and Mom were gone this morning; they were busy trying to build a house to get me settled. Everyday Dad and Larry would work on the new house as soon as daylight broke; then Dad would go to his job as a river warden with the provincial department of fisheries; then he would come back and work on the house until dark. Mom went with them and stayed there to do what she could with Larry while Dad was gone to work, and then she stayed with Dad until it was dark and they couldn't do anything else with the house. On the weekends they spent the entire day there and Neil would join them. They were anxious to have a place for me to stay when I was finished with the hospital.

Before they rebuilt, on the second or third week after the fire and before starting the foundation, Dad had asked Mom to ask me where I wanted to live. I had said I couldn't imagine being anywhere else but in our own yard. I didn't realize that it had been left up to me, that whatever I said was what was going to be done, according to Dad. They poured the basement for the new house a short time later, just a few feet in front of where the old house had stood.

People were so good to our family. Most people in North Harbour and many in the neighbouring communities volunteered their time, their services, and local businesses their supplies to help out as much as they could. The house was well underway before I got back.

This was how life went on. People went back to work. But I came home for the first time not having moved past day one. And, for the most part, denying there was ever a day one. Sometimes I still believed that this was a dream; it was now getting to be a long dream, but still, I hoped, a dream.

My first encounter with the disconnection to "what used to be" came a little while later. I had my breakfast of tea and home-made toast that my grandmother was so anxious to provide. She wanted to cook more for me but that was all I wanted. I talked with my grandparents for a while and then shuffled into a pair of sneakers my mom had bought before slowly making my way up the road.

My nan said that my mother was coming back for me but I was too anxious to wait. It was early – just past 8am – and I wanted to see the changes in the full light of day. It was about a ten-minute walk for me to get up the road because I was so weak that after I took a few steps I needed a break. I made my way, leaning on the guardrail on the side of the road, and then in the distance I saw my mother coming the other way to meet me.

I was so happy to see her, and though she was mad that I had not waited she smiled just the same and linked her arm in mine for support as I walked. People came out of their houses and waved and greeted me. The people of North Harbour were amazing.

When we got to the graveyard I told Mom I was not ready to go in. I wanted to see the inside of the new house and how it was going first. That was only a few steps further.

There was a small fire pit outside the new house in the rocks where Mom cooked some meals during the day in the old iron frying pan that had been salvaged from the burned house – one of the few things that had been. We walked in through the basement door in the back of the house and all the framing was in place and the floor was ready for cement. A ladder was set up to get up to the main level, which I was not strong enough to attempt, so I was only able to look up from the rocks beneath.

Floor plans were on an old yellow table set in the gravel and I eyed them to imagine what would be above me when the house was finished. Dad, Neil and Larry came down from somewhere above and gave me a hug. We hung around for a while; I sat and rested on a makeshift chair as Mom went about doing some tasks with the others. She kept coming back to check on me every few minutes even though I told her I was fine.

After resting for a while, I got up going toward the door as I listened to the voices and the sounds of the hammers pounding diligently above. I wandered outside, looking over at the stable still standing as if nothing happened. I decided to have a look around, crossing the little stick bridge Dad had always kept on the river that dissected the property.

The day was bright and sunny, not unlike the last day I was here. I climbed the couple of steps to the door of the shed attached to the front of the stable, struggled to turn the old rusty knob, and then pushed it open. The bandage that wrapped around my thumb turned an orangey-brown as I strained to turn the knob.

Nothing had changed in here. The homemade table tennis table was still on the floor resting on two metal trunks. I could see Sharon on the other end as we knelt down to play our many games. The table was made of two separate pieces of plywood, neither one square nor the same size. We each had an end that we knelt at because the other end was too weird when we changed, so we kept it the same. I was by the door; she was by the back window.

On sunny days like this the shed was cool. Flies buzzed against the windows and I could see the dust that I had just disturbed in the framed light streaming into the old musty shed. We spent a lot of happy days here; we would probably be here today if things had not changed. When some of our friends came over we pushed away the trunks and played house there with our dolls. Pretend food, pretend parties, and pretend children; all pretend and no longer possible. Maybe that life had not been real, that had been the dream. I was confused trying to focus. It was a lot to take in at one time.

I left the comfort of the shed and went back towards the house. I slowly walked to, and stood on, the gravel where our other house had been. There was no sign that anything bad had happened there, just some dirt and rocks and clay.

Where is my world, where has it gone?

This was so unbelievable that I couldn't take it all in. With the exception of the old red ochre stable, nothing was like it was before.

Mom came looking for me and I said I was ready to go to the graveyard if she could go with me. We took our time and slowly made our way back the dirt road. I was getting very tired by now and was slowly hunching over into a semi-fetal protective position that I normally forced myself not to do. Today it was comforting.

The lane up through the center of the graveyard was a little steep and took my breath away. I looked to the right and there was a large patch of earth that looked out of place. It was barren and bleak: five white crosses stood out on the dark earth.

My mother started to cry as we edged our way across the grass. I bit into the insides of my cheeks so that I would not cry. As we got closer and closer to the gravesite I could feel the weight of her leaning on me more and more. I was tired and weak but I forced myself to pull out all the strength I could get to support her across the last few steps.

I stared at the crosses in silence, listening to my mother trying to compose herself and, strangely, the birds singing. How could the birds be singing when this was so sad? How could there be anything joyful or musical in this sad place? I felt like shouting at the birds to shut up, but I did not.

I started to ask Mom questions about that day of the funeral so I could picture in my mind what had happened. Every now and again I would get a thought flickering through my mind that this could be a dream, there would be a waking point – though I knew that was not possible. The world had gone on, family and community had progressed through the grieving process, and I was alone with mine – while avoiding letting my mother see that I was not strong on the inside. Nobody had mentioned the fire since I came home because it was too painful for the whole community and especially for my family.

It was odd for me; this whole thing seemed like a bad movie and it was hard to distinguish reality. This was my mother, beside me in the graveyard. I had spent the first night of my life at my grandparents' house. My whole life that used to be was no more. I couldn't grieve, it was not in me. I couldn't cry, except for the sadness I felt for my mother and my family – I felt no sadness for myself.

I guess I believed if I grieved it would make this insanity true and if I didn't cry there was a possibility that I would be transported back to June 18th. Half of my family was beneath my feet in this dirt that was out of place in the landscape of grass and various types of headstones. I desperately needed a rewind button to make it all go away.

As I backed away from the graves I noticed Jackie Dalton's headstone nearer to the road a few steps away. I was taken aback when I realized that she had died only six months before the fire. I could remember being at her wake on the south side of North Harbour and I distinctly remembered being a little girl at that time. I was no longer that little girl now and would never be that innocent again.

One of our neighbours stopped for us as we were leaving the graveyard and brought us back to my grandparents' house. We had a lunch and then I rested upstairs for a couple of hours before visiting Marg and Dick and their family, and then going back to the Shop that evening. There was a little bit of joy and comfort at the Shop, and it was safe and I liked it there. The routine was set for my days back home. I went to the new house in the morning, rested, to the Shop in the evening and then back to my grandparents' for bed.

Sunday came and I had to go back to the city to create a "St. John's" routine. Yvonne and Jeff had graciously offered me a room at their house and they lived close to the hospital. The offer was for as long as I needed it; at this point, we had no idea what that would be. Mary wanted me to stay with her; however, she was living with some girl friends in a rental and was already sharing her room so Yvonne's was the best choice.

The first week's schedule was bandage changes and physio every morning at the hospital and then back to Yvonne's to rest. She and Jeff worked during the day so I puttered around the house trying to do whatever little housework I could. They were adamant that I do nothing but it helped pass the time. I wanted to try to stay mobile.

Each morning I called a cab to come get me so I could go to the hospital. After the first couple of times, the taxi driver, just making conversation, asked what I was doing at the hospital. I explained what I had to do every day and what had happened to me.

He was silent for a little while and then he told me not to call for a taxi the next morning. He said he would be at the house for me at 8am to bring me to the hospital. When we arrived at the hospital the next morning he wouldn't take my money. He asked how long I would be inside and I said I wasn't sure. He told me to call and request his car number and if he was near he would bring me home. An hour later I called and he was there outside the hospital doors, and he never charged me to bring me home either.

Next day, sure enough, the same cab driver was there to pick me up and bring me to the hospital and again would not take any payment. I asked him why he wouldn't take any money and explained that my mom had allotted money for the taxis when I was leaving on Sunday. He said that I was around the same age as his granddaughter and he hoped that if she were in the situation I was in somebody would help her like he was helping me.

So for the rest of my time in St. John's the cab driver brought me back and forth to the hospital at no charge. When my "regular driver" was not able to pick me up, somebody else would show up and each time it was no charge. They were very good to me and I never had to wait.

The next weekend was Labour Day weekend and it meant I would get three days home because the clinics were closed on Monday. The nurses at the clinic gave me bandages and tape in case some of mine came off before my Tuesday visit.

A taxi service had started between St. Mary's Bay and St. John's every weekday so I was given a spot on the taxi to get back and forth for the weekends. I was dropped off at my grandparents' house late that Friday night, the first of many. I visited my aunt and uncle's house, the Shop, our new house under construction and the graveyard: my routine was set and that was all I could hope for. Life was really one day at a time, take what comes, and make the best of it. I had no other expectations because that was all I could handle. One day at a time was not so bad and was a better deal than what Francis, Richard, Sharon, Harold or Barry had gotten.

One day during the week, I had a visit from a police officer, who questioned me about the fire. As standard protocol I was asked to relive the events of June 19th. I told him the story as if it were that – a story. I never shed a tear or faltered as I spoke. He made notes as I was speaking and asked me a few questions. He must have been satisfied with the answers, but as he was leaving he said that there would be a judicial enquiry held and that I would have to go to court. That too was standard protocol.

The next weekend was close to my birthday, September 11th; and I would be sixteen. School had started that week without me and I missed that. To make me smile, the community decided to have a surprise birthday/welcome home party for me in the Community Hall.

There would be (I was told), a Sock Hop for the little ones, starting at 6pm, followed by a teen dance at 9:30 pm, which wasn't uncommon on a Saturday night in the community but would have normally been on the long weekend – the Labour Day weekend the week before.

Mom told me to go to the early dance because I would be tired later. I always loved spending time with the little ones so I did not mind going. I had babysat most of the kids that would be there and I looked forward to seeing them.

When I walked into the Community Hall there was a wall of faces, young and old, and everyone shouted out, "Surprise!" I was shocked. Music blasted all the top hits and everyone formed lines to talk to me. They didn't want to crowd me in case I got hurt.

The next hour went by in a blur. As everyone tried to speak to me, I noticed people had come from outside North Harbour as well: some of the teachers from school, some kids from other communities, classmates, people I didn't know at all but who my parents must have known – I was overwhelmed.

A cake with sixteen candles appeared. Adults sat on the chairs and the benches on each side of the community hall and most of the young people knelt on the floor in concentric circles with a place for me in the middle. "Happy Birthday" was sung and shouted to the rafters. After I blew out the candles, some of the older teenagers helped me get down on my knees in the center of the mass of people.

I never in my wildest dreams could have envisioned the gifts that kept coming my way. Some of my friends had to help rip the paper and show me what I had received. There were so many gifts of clothing, with my favourite being a pair of red jeans from my Grade 11 class at Our Lady of Mount Carmel. I had very little clothing with the exception of some loose fitting stuff to help me get through the hospital visits and the weekends. There was so much money as well; it was hundreds and hundreds of dollars – over $500. I had never had any amount of money in my life and this was so amazing.

When the party was over I wanted my mom to take the money to help build the house but she refused and said that the money was for me to splurge on myself. She told me to go the mall when I was stronger and buy myself some nice things.

The party continued and kids from my school all told me how much they missed me. This would be my last year of high school and it should have been my best year. I would not pity myself but I did wish that I could be in school with them so that things could go back to the way they were in some respects. In a way, I had left the community in June as a little girl and had returned as a grown-up. I felt so much older in such a short time.

When I was going back to St. John's the next day my mother gave me money for the week as she had done the two weeks prior. I told her I had money and she said that the birthday money was for me and me alone, and that I should spend it on myself.

She also told me that I would have to start going to school in St. John's. She said I had no choice because nobody could be sure how long I would be in St. John's and that arrangements had been made for me to go to Holy Heart High School the next day. She said all my books and everything would be given to me when I got there and that Yvonne would take me for my first day.

On Monday I dressed in my red jeans, which were a little too big, as small as they were, and another birthday shirt that covered almost all the white dressings. Yvonne brought me to the hospital to get the bandages changed and do my physio and then she drove me to Holy Heart for my first day of school. I had been foolish enough to think that nothing else could affect me anymore because I was so immune to change by this time, but was I ever wrong.

When we pulled up to the school I just stared at the multi-storey building – it was surreal. I asked Yvonne how many kids went here to school and she told me it was probably around a thousand and they were all girls. My eyes bulged when she told me and she laughed out loud. Our Lady of Mount Carmel, my all-grade school from Grades 1 to 11, had about three hundred students in total and this one had over three hundred girls in Grade 11 alone.

We walked in, she brought me to the office where I was given my books and I was told to go to a classroom number on the third floor. I noticed that it was all very detached and impersonal, like I was nothing but a bother from the ordinary.

Yvonne said goodbye and left me just before the bell rang for recess. The doors flew open all along the first floor and students piled into the hall and I was in the middle of chaos.

I was bumped and pushed and stared at and whispered about as people moved here and there throughout the building. I saw some double doors to the stairs and I moved in the stairwell where there was less "people traffic." I slowly climbed the stairs taking rests after five or six steps. I had to go up two more floors and by the time I got to the top the bell was sounding to end recess. There were students and teachers going up and down the stairs but they avoided me as best as possible.

The hall was empty now on the third floor and I looked around for the room number where I needed to be. It was halfway up the long corridor and I made my way slowly with an arm full of books. With the exception of the hospital, I had never seen such an enormous place. I was very tired by this time and very nervous. My old school would have welcoming smiling faces; this one had a sea of unfamiliar girls who were not the least bit friendly from what I could tell. However, it was early yet and I needed to give it time.

When I knocked on the slightly opened door the teacher waved for me to come in. I hesitantly walked across the front of the class of thirty-five or so girls and presented myself to the teacher. I had to be a sight in beautiful red jeans pulled on over a skeleton, with short hair, blotchy skin and bumps and red marks on my face and all over where you could see. The room was silent as the teacher asked me who I was. I told her my name and said I was a new student.

Before I could say anything more she said that I was late and needed a note from the office. I asked what did that mean and she said to go to the first floor office and ask the secretary for a note.

She said she didn't know how they handled lateness in my other school but it was unacceptable here. I needed the late slip before being granted access to the class.

I was raised to do as I was told so I turned to leave the class and could hear the snickering and whispers from the students as I made my way back across the room. I was not going to like this at all and had not made a great first impression. I went back down the stairs to ask for a note at the office and returned to climb the stairs again. The secretary said I didn't need a note because it was my first day but she gave me one anyway. It was almost a half an hour before I got back to the room and knocked again before entering. I was weary by this time and the teacher beckoned me to come in. She said, "Hurry up there now as the class is almost over."

She took the note and showed me a desk at the very front of the class. I didn't even know what class I was in so I couldn't select the correct book. By the time I figured it out the bell was ringing and everyone in the class got up to leave with the exception of me.

The teacher stared at me and asked why I was still there. I asked what she meant. In my old school we never changed class-rooms, the teachers came to us. Not so at Holy Heart. The teacher said I had to change classes and she called to one of the last girls exiting the room to come back and show me to my next class.

I was grateful to the girl who came back. She asked me where I was from and I told her North Harbour. She asked if that was in Newfoundland and I said yes. She asked if I had a class schedule and I said that I thought I did. As we entered the crowded corridor she asked if I had a locker and I said no so she brought me to her locker and showed me the schedule on the inside of the door and told me that the numbers at the bottom of each time slot corre-lated with the classrooms we were expected to be in. I thanked her and she said I really should get a locker. She told me it was now lunchtime so I slowly headed back down the stairs to ask for a locker.

By the time I got back up to the third floor with my books to my new locker, lunch was over. Where to now? The girl who had shown me the schedule before lunch passed by and pointed to the book I needed and the class I was to go to. She said to hurry or I would be late. I thanked her as I pushed the books in and grabbed the one I needed for the next class. When the day's last bell rang I was exhausted and ready to go back to Yvonne's.

When Yvonne and Jeff got home they both asked me how it was and I said it had gone alright but it really had not. After bandages the next day I told the taxi driver I had to go to school so he took me there instead of the house. He asked me how I ended up at Holy Heart and I said I had no idea but that I had to go to school. He wished me luck.

I went to the office when I got in and said I needed a late slip for class and the secretary told me that I didn't need one because I had been at the hospital and it would be part of my routine. I went to the class I was required to be in and another teacher asked me for a late slip. I told her the secretary said I didn't need one and she said yes I did (as if she didn't believe me) and to go back down and get one. I turned and went back downstairs again and the secretary said she didn't know why I needed one but she gave it to me anyway.

The class was almost over by the time I got back. Again, I heard the snickers and felt the stares as I sat down again in the front. I was trying to blend in but was not doing a good job of it. I had brought money for lunch that day but didn't find the cafeteria until lunch was almost over. I was so glad when the day was finished.

The next day I asked the secretary for a note again and she said again I didn't need one, so this time I went up and waited by the locker until the class was over and I joined in the next class after the bell. I still had to sit at the front of class. There was no friend material at this school and everybody seemed to avoid me.

I remembered a couple of occasions when a new student had come to my old school; the teacher introduced them and told us all to make the student welcome. By the end of the first day we had all made a point to go see the person and get to know them. Here was so different. I was very alone, more alone than I was at the hospital even on days when I had no visitors. The whole week of school was a nightmare; I did not want to be there at all. I refused to cry about it and tried to be strong but the experience was wearing on me.

My sixteenth birthday was on Thursday and nobody recognized it at school – *Why would they though?* I wondered. That evening Yvonne and Jeff had a cake for me, Neil asked me to go to the Avalon Mall and Mary said she would meet us there, and my parents called. The day was not a total write-off, but not what a sixteenth birthday should have been. How I wished I was back in the comfort of my community and my school.

As I walked through the mall with Neil I could sense that he was not comfortable with how people were looking at me. I couldn't blame them because I was this scrawny hunched over person with blotchy red marks on my face and I stood out. I was walking rather slowly because it was really tiring and some older lady came up to me and asked what happened. Before I could say anything Neil told her it was none of her business and it was rude to stare at people. That was how it went for the next hour and it was funny in a way because Neil almost growled at people to stop looking at me, although I told him I didn't mind. We met up with Mary and had something to eat before going back to the safety of Yvonne and Jeff's house.

That weekend I told my mother that school was hard and how I was late every day. She said it would get better if I gave it time.

The next week did not get better. I had tried to start up a conversation with people in my class but unlike home, the same people were not in my class every time. I was ostracised as a freak because of my appearance, and nobody wanted to be associated with me. I was retreating further and further into a shell and every day it got worse. As hard as I tried to be strong, I could feel that it wasn't enough. I would not go out in the evening because it was too hard. People were cruel whether they meant to be or not.

That weekend I told my parents that I did not want to go to school anymore and to see if there was anything they could do to get me out of it. Mom told me I had to go back until something was settled.

On Monday after the bandage change I had my weekly visit with Dr. Anderson. He told me I needed surgery again and that he would fit me in on Wednesday. He said I wouldn't be admitted, that I could go home the same day. He got permission from my parents to do the operation and it was set for 7am. I was happy because it meant I didn't have to go to school for a few days. At least I knew what to expect by now with surgery, I could handle that pain.

I went to school Monday and Tuesday and things were going downhill. I was pointed at and laughed at and made fun of so many times. I was bumped and my books knocked down. I had no friends there, and knew I had to plead my case to my parents not to go back.

My surgery on Wednesday was as expected and, after resting at Yvonne's for the first few days, I was allowed to briefly go home to North Harbour to recoup. The graft site was my right leg again and I wasn't allowed to walk around until the skin set. Yvonne and Jeff brought me out to North Harbour again that Friday. During my few days at home I convinced my mother to call my old school to see what they could do for me. She did and was greeted by a very different attitude than that of the large school in St. John's.

The principal, who was new this year, said that she and all the teachers were looking forward to my return. When Mom explained what I had been going through at Holy Heart, she told my mother she would work out a plan. By Monday it was all set. I didn't have to go back to Holy Heart unless I wanted and if I was discharged from the daily hospital visits in time for me to finish my Grade 11 and graduate with my class they would do everything possible to make it happen. Because I still couldn't hold a pen for long periods of time, the principal said she would make sure I got notes for anything that could possibly be on the final public exams.

After a week at home I was back to Yvonne's again for my daily dressings and physio. The same cab driver showed up to bring me for the bandage change when I called. I told him I didn't have to go back to school in St. John's and he said he was so happy for me because he could see in my face how much it hurt me to go there. I was finished with Holy Heart and those few weeks of misery were behind me. I could concentrate on getting better.

The surgery had went well and Dr. Anderson, as always, said I was an amazing healer. He was very pleased with my progress. I was able to have dressing changes less often now and on Monday, Tuesday and Thursday, meaning I could go home on Thursdays now instead of Fridays.

I concentrated on my physiotherapy and tried to do the exercises several times a day instead of the required one. I didn't want to overdo it but I knew what my body could handle and I wanted to get back to school to graduate with my classmates – that was my plan. That one thing in my life could be under my control if I worked hard enough.

The second Friday I was home I had been invited to go to school for the day and sit with my class. I was so excited when I got up to catch the bus. I wore my red jeans, which fit me a little better now as I was starting to gain some weight.

My cousins met me at my grandparents' house and walked me up to their bus stop. The bus arrived and students who were already on the bus from further down the Harbour cheered as I was helped up the steep steps by one of my cousins. The bus driver said he knew I was coming and saved the front seat for me by myself so that I would not get hurt. Everyone was so respectful and caring.

When I got to school the entire school population of North Harbour all waited for me to make my way to the doors and escorted me in. The principal brought me into her office and told me to wait there until the corridors cleared so that I would be safe. Teachers came out of the teachers' lounge and said hello, asking questions about how I was and how things were going. I answered as best I could and then my Grade 11 homeroom teacher escorted me to class when the first bell rang.

As I walked into the classroom I could see the faces light up and everyone was so excited to see me. Some students from the bus had said I was in school and they were waiting patiently for me to arrive. The loudspeaker buzzed for the usual morning announcements and the first one was, "Ida Linehan is in school today, please everyone make her welcome and be careful around her." Then I heard a burst of applause from the speaker and the classrooms across the hall and whoops and hollers. Wow, that was so cool to be welcomed like that. I smiled for the first time in a long time from the inside.

The class remained quiet for the rest of the announcements and then everyone sat there and looked at me where I stood with the teacher. He asked me if I would like to say anything and I shook my head to say no. He understood and laughed saying that was a nice change and said that my desk was waiting for me to return.

Sure enough there was a desk with my books on it, right in front of my best friend Georgette Pieroway's. I sat in front of Georgette every year and my place was still there if I could get back for the rest of the school year. Georgette had the biggest smile of the bunch and she patted the back of the desk for me to sit.

Before the class started the teacher showed me which book we were using and where we were in the book and said that I could follow along if I wanted or just sit there and be with the class. I, being a diligent student, followed along and even answered some questions posed to the class. This is where I wanted to be, nothing had changed here and I was more determined than ever to get back. Two weeks later I got back for another day and it made me so happy.

In late October, I was measured for Jobst (compression) Garments – tightly-fitted zippered clothing that would press on the protruding scars and help reduce them over time. These were very expensive but Mom and Dad said not to worry about that, they would take care of it. I had two suits ordered.

When I got home that week I had a great surprise. The house was finished and we could move in. Halloween Night we had treats for the kids and spent our first night at the new house. We didn't have all the furniture but we did have a couple of beds. Saturday, November 1st I went with my mom and my grandmother on a furniture-buying trip.

My nan and grandfather had saved money to get me a bedroom set; she wanted to come with me to pick it out. That and other furniture was delivered during the week and when I got home the next weekend everything was set up in the new house in what should have been a joyous occasion.

It wasn't!

Mom and Dad had received a small amount of life insurance for Francis, who had been working with the provincial government for about a year when he died. When the money came, Dad found out the amount of the bill for the funeral that had been paid for by the welfare system, took that amount out of Francis' life insurance and sent the money to the social services office in St. Mary's. He felt obligated to pay for Francis' funeral and told Mom that Francis would have wanted to pay for the others, so they did. Dad never wanted to be indebted to anyone. They bought some furniture with the rest of the money and paid off Richard's and Francis' student loans.

By mid-November the Jobst Garments had arrived and I had to wear the gloves and upper body clothing at all times. My face had healed enough that a mask was not necessary. There were still some bulking scars on my nose and jaw but they too were shrinking on their own and the blotchy appearance would abate over time.

The garments were very itchy and constrictive but had to be worn and I would tolerate it as long as I needed to wear them. I could notice the difference in the scarring when I removed them to have dressings changed. Mom hand-washed them while I was home on the weekends and hung them over the woodstove to dry.

My dressings were getting smaller and smaller as the open wounds healed and the skin grafts took. I was progressing faster than expected, according to Dr. Anderson. By December 16th my physio efforts had paid off and I was discharged from therapy. I had as much movement as they felt I would get and I had been doing the exercises on my own for so long that I had exceeded their requirements. I met with a social worker who asked me a couple of questions before deeming that I had adjusted well to the loss and needed no more counselling. I never realized that I had had any to begin with so I must be doing amazing.

On Wednesday December 17th, 1980, 181 days after being admitted, I was officially discharged from the hospital. My bandages came off for the last time and I needed no more daily dressings. I would be home for Christmas.

I had always loved Christmas, who didn't as a child? We never had very much money but we always had a great Christmas growing up. I remembered a couple of years before when myself and Sharon had gotten some old cardboard boxes and made a life-size chimney and fireplace. We coloured each brick with red crayons, and around the bricks we coloured black. It took us over a month to finish, and then we decorated it for Christmas with tinsel and hung our stockings on the makeshift fireplace that year. Dad even cut up a few smaller pieces of wood to make it more real. Mom was so proud of the construction that it took a place of honor in the living room near the tree and she showed it to everyone that visited. And in what had become a tradition we had homemade pizzas on Christmas Eve before going to bed and ate them in front of the fireplace.

Myself and Sharon, along with the younger boys, always made a little house under the woodpile by the corner of the fence. We would bar off a small square between the fence and the woodpile, where we would put up a Christmas tree. The tree always had egg carton ornaments and a paper chain garland; it was a sight to behold. We would be so proud of that every year and got tea and brought it out there to have Christmas tea parties.

How would we ever get back to Christmas in our new house? Mom was adamant that there would be no decorations and no tree this year. She said, "There was nothing to celebrate so therefore there would be no celebrations."

My poor parents, their life was so empty. They had spent all their physical time building a house to keep their minds off their loss and that was done now. They had spent all their emotional time focusing on my getting better and I was home now. Time had caught up with them – they had time to think, time to do nothing and they were not doing well.

I believed if they had no Christmas this year, they would never have Christmas again. I knew that and I didn't want that for them. If they could get through it this first year I believed they would have a greater chance to heal. Usually parents had time to adjust to Christmas with dwindling numbers of children, but they did not. It was all or nothing for them this year.

I told Mom that I needed to have Christmas for my own state of mind. I couldn't handle an empty sadness in such a time of peacefulness and happiness. There were decorations everywhere I went – the school, the Shop, my uncle's and even my grandparents had up a few decorations, although not many. Mom said she would not relent; there would be no Christmas in the house, ever.

I said Christmas would come whether we wanted it or not. I also said that I wouldn't stay in the new house without a Christmas tree. I told her I would go to my uncle Dick's, or somewhere else that had a tree. I became stubborn on this issue, which was so unlike me. When had Christmas become an issue? When had I gotten stubborn?

Finally she said that we could have a small tree in the living room and I was happy with that. I knew that I would get my way because they would do anything for me. I had manipulated the situation, however I wasn't doing this to hurt them, but hoped I was helping in some way. Over the next few days myself, Larry and Neil cut a tree and Mom gave me money to buy some decorations at the Shop.

Mom would not go in the living room at first. Dad did. Gradually I coaxed her in to look at the tree pretending I needed her help to straighten it up, or some such excuse.

We were all very sad, it was not a happy time. It was hard but it was necessary. There were a couple of gifts under the tree but not many and that was fine, it was not about the gifts but about the experience.

Mom's godchild came in on Christmas Eve to give her a gift. She never spoke but put her arms around him and cried and cried. He didn't know what to do but put his arms around her and held her until she could speak. As a teenager, it was very brave of him to come as most people were not so brave. The neighbours didn't know whether to visit or not, what to say, what to do. Mom or Dad never visited anyone either. Nobody knew how to handle it. I still believed that it was best to have a Christmas tree or next year would have been twice as hard. It was depressing but it was a start.

My uncle Dick and his wife Marg made regular visits, as did Jose and Seb and Thomas and Mrs. Catherine Dalton, and they continued to do that over the Christmas season.

Like me, Larry and Neil did not enjoy it and Eddy didn't come home. New Year's Eve we spent playing cards to pass the time. I was sure glad to be rid of 1980.

In January, I was back in school with my class. This was normal and I was so glad to have it. I started in January doing the September work and by the time late February came around I had caught up with the rest of the class.

I had had several doctor's appointments and I was progressing nicely. I continued to wear the Jobst Garments but they, along with my body's natural healing process, made me very itchy. Georgette had her hand permanently across the top of her desk gently scratching my back to give me some relief. Mom would do the same thing for me at home. At school picture time I tried to hide the unsightly garments and gloves beneath the white graduation robe and red flowers. Even simple things were always complicated and never easy.

When final exam time came I was prepared, I had worked hard. School exams were written before the school year ended and then the Grade 11s would have to do public exams. The school had class parties and an awards night the last day of school before the Publics, and my mother and I were invited.

Our family had always been invited to awards night for academic and sports awards. On the way to the awards ceremony my mom talked about the year before when all three of us – me, Sharon, and Harold – were invited to the high school. The whole night Harold kept telling Mom that it must be a mistake that he was there. Finally they called his name and he had gotten honours marks for Grade 7. He was so happy. The next day he was gone.

Barry was always smart, almost brilliant. He was doing some high school curriculum while in elementary school. I had often heard the story of Barry's first day of Kindergarten. The teachers were trying to assess where each of the kids were in their development and one of the tasks was to say an animal and then spell it. Most of the kids would say cat or dog and some could spell the word and some could not.

When it came to Barry's turn they asked him to name an animal and he said, "Hippopotamus," so for fun they asked him to spell it, never expecting that he could. He did, correctly – the teacher had to make sure by looking it up in the dictionary. Barry flourished in the lower grades and was given more challenging work as he moved up.

Both myself and Sharon had always gotten invited to awards nights as well, we had academic and sports achievements every year. Sharon was a great cross-country runner and excelled at any of the sprints or short distance races. She won awards for table tennis and badminton, volleyball and most of the other sports that were offered at the school. She always won awards for top marks as well in many subjects. Every year she brought home loads of trophies and medals from awards night.

This year was the last one for our family. There would be no more. I thought I was only there as a token gesture because for the first time ever I was not able to achieve honours that year. However, when it came time to announce the Student of the Year my name was called and the audience rose and cheered. I was embarrassed and thought I was undeserving but graciously accepted the award as offered. It was an honour to be chosen and I was just so glad to have made it.

I did it; I graduated after a horrible year, with my classmates that I had been with since Grade 1. It was quite an accomplishment considering I only had a few months to do it. My parents were proud of what I had done and were so happy for me. That few months at school had given my soul a chance to begin the healing process and brought back a little bit of the old me. I was grateful.

I spent the summer recuperating and regaining some of my strength. I started to be a little more active, however my burns were very constrictive and kept me from being as energetic as I would have been. No matter what, I felt safe here. My friends were genuine and didn't stare. They asked questions making sure I was OK but never made me feel anything negative. I had somewhere I belonged.

I wanted to go swimming with the rest of the gang from North Harbour so my mother bought me a bodysuit suitable for a gymnast with long sleeves to help protect me from the sun. Swimming at a hole in Cape Dog River was a tradition after the swimming area on the Flat's River had washed out. The water was cool but on a hot day it was nice to go for a dip with the crowd. I could not swim very well but any movement was great and everyone looked out for me making sure I was doing OK.

I remembered when we were younger Dad had created a salt-water pool during low tide by piling up large beach rocks out in the Atlantic Ocean in front of our house. When the tide came in he allowed us to go and play in the water as long as our older brothers were with us and as long as we didn't go "out of bounds" or outside the rock wall. Every day we went swimming and sometimes Dad came with us. So many good memories of childhood!

When September came, all my high school classmates were heading off to college and I was not. With all the commotion of the last year of high school I had not thought about "what I wanted to be when I grew up." Ironic as it seemed there was the possibility that I would not have grown up and now I had.

After the first week had passed Mom and Dad asked me if I would like be a civil engineer like Francis, and knowing my cousin Marie had also completed the course a few years before I said yes. I believed that both my parents wanted me to do this even though I had no idea what it entailed or what I would work at or where I would work. I liked school and I had enjoyed my last few months at my high school so I thought I would be able to be where my friends were as most of my classmates were in St. John's in college or university.

I don't know who pulled what strings but the following Monday I was supposed to go to the College of Trades and Technology where I had enrolled in Civil Engineering Technology – a two year program that had started classes two weeks prior. I was going to stay with Jose's son and daughter who were also in school in St. John's and could come home on the weekends with them as well. Everything fell into place.

On Monday I entered the college for the first time. Structurally it was reminiscent of the high school I had attended for the few weeks exactly a year before. I chose to ignore that thought, believing that there was no way this could be as bad.

I wore long sleeved clothing which helped cover up most of my burns and kept me from being a freak in the eyes of the school population. When I got my books and started towards my locker, passing through the double doors and approaching my class, I noticed that there was not one female to be seen. Not good.

I went in the classroom with a bunch of guys and asked if there was a particular place I should sit. I ended up in the front as most of the rear seats were taken. When the teacher came in he looked around at all the class and said that there was a girl who was going to try her hand in a "man's course." Everyone laughed except me. This really was not going to be good.

The teacher kept making derogatory remarks regarding girls in engineering every chance he got. With the exception of one or two teachers, this was how each class went. I was miserable. There were only ten minutes between each class and I never got to go see my friends on the other wing of the school so it was a very lonely place.

I was laughed at and picked on by the teachers and most of the students. Some would pretend to be friendly and would put signs on my back or rub my face with pencil lead or anything nasty to try and get me to leave the program. I couldn't leave because I didn't want to disappoint my parents. I was stuck.

Every evening I would go to the mall and walk around, go back to the apartment, do my homework, and when my roommates were in bed I would cry. I played John Denver's "Some Days Are Diamonds (some days are stones)" over and over as I lay on the carpet and wept. Life was not supposed to be this difficult all the time. When was I going to get a break? I felt so sorry for myself and I was stuck.

Every Wednesday a bursary would arrive at the school for most of the students and our homeroom teacher would deliver the cheques. These had our first name, the first three letters of our middle name and our last name printed in the window of the envelope. My middle name was Fatima so this read Ida Fat Linehan.

Every time he brought in the cheque, the teacher would get to mine and shout out "Fat Linehan" and the class would go in an uproar of laughter because I was so gaunt and scrawny. I would be embarrassed and turn red as I went to take it from his hands. Blushing made the burns on my face more noticeable and that would make them laugh even more. I would be mortified, but I felt I had to stick with it for my parent's sake.

Each morning as I entered the school and walked down towards K wing I had to run the gauntlet through the all-male mechanical wing. People threw down their books in front of me, intentionally bumped me, pushed me, and sometimes tried to trip me. Mostly they were cruel.

There was nobody to hang out with so I went from class to class by myself and sat in the front at all times. I was out of my element as well because although the male students could go to the teachers to ask for help, I felt I could not. I also had numerous doctors' appointments, which delayed me and put me behind. I worked hard but was not getting great grades.

One of the students, our class president, was very genuine, at least I thought he was, and he was very nice to me. He tried to include me in class things when most of the class didn't want me; he waited for me to get my books and offered assistance whenever he could. I liked that he was trying.

One morning while getting off the bus, I noticed that the flag was half-mast at the school. It was very rare to see this. By the time I got to my locker I heard from the whispering of people around me that somebody from our wing of the school had died. Our class was unusually quiet when I got in there that morning and the teacher came in to tell us that one of our classmates had perished in a house fire the night before. It was our class president. I went into a state of shock. My heart raced; my stomach did a somersault. There was no way this could have happened. He was so nice to me. Images of my family passed before my eyes.

I tuned into the teacher again as he continued to say that this was the second time that he had lost a student through a fire in the last few years. He said he had a student named Francis Linehan who had graduated from Civil a few years before, and then he looked at me and asked if he was related to me.

I managed to croak out that he was my brother. I stared straight ahead and had my back straight as I sat there and endured the stares from the class. How could this be happening? It just wasn't fair.

My only sort of friend in the class was gone, the taunts continued and life became unbearable. A few of the guys in the class who had been very shy in the beginning tried to help me out a little for the duration of the school year, but there was nobody any happier than I was when the first year was over.

For the first time in my life I had failed one of the subjects and had to repeat it. It was a wonder I had passed anything at all.

I worked on a student program in North Harbour that summer and was happy to get back to a safe place for a few months. Then September came and I dreaded going back to school, but I had to for my parent's sake. I had no way of knowing that life was not this hard for everybody. I didn't talk about anything. I covered up my burns so that I wouldn't stand out any more than being the only girl on K-wing made me stand out.

Alone, miserable: I was the ultimate victim, and the more I thought of myself that way, the more I lived as a victim. Life was hard for everyone – that is what I knew. My parents had it hard; my siblings had it hard; I had it hard. That was normal and I had to make the best of it – in my head, I attracted victimization.

School was not any harder than the year before and being able to start class at the beginning of the semester allowed me to get the foundation of each course under me. I hadn't realized how important that was the year before when I came in two weeks late. This year was a bit easier: not nice or enjoyable but a bit easier.

After three weeks I had my regular visit with Dr. Anderson. He said I had to go for surgery and that I would be admitted the next morning. I didn't have much time to prepare but was so glad to get out of class for a couple of weeks that I jumped at the opportunity. I notified my teacher that afternoon and he never said good luck, can I help you get schoolwork, nothing. I did not expect any better as I was a girl in a "man's world."

The next morning bright and early I was at the hospital and was sent to surgery almost immediately. Dr. Anderson said it might take a while. I had severe keloid scarring that had to be removed and skin grafts. The graft area was my right thigh and when I got back from surgery I learned that I had a lot of bleeding from that site. I had several bags of blood and had to stay in bed for three days. My mother came to see me after surgery and stayed in St. John's for a few days until I could get out of bed.

One good thing was that I could stay on a ward, which meant I had roommates. A girl, a little older than I was, was in the bed across from me. We struck up a conversation and became immediate friends. For the next three weeks we hung out together and explored the hospital at night when everyone was gone to bed. It was actually fun to be able to do that. I almost felt like the child that I had been before all this chaos happened.

I went to see if there was a Burn Unit anymore and sure enough a man in his early thirties had come in and was its lone occupant, much like I had been. He had an electrical burn to his chest and was in an extreme amount of pain.

Rusty told me that I was the benchmark for all patients in the Burn Unit and nobody lived up to me yet. She was such a sweetheart. She was also out on my ward for some shifts and every time I walked up or down the corridor when she was working I would hear her shouting, "Ida Linehan, you straighten up now and don't be hunching over!" She was right, I had to force myself to walk straighter so that my grafts could heal and give me stretch room.

When I was able to get out of the ward, Rusty came in to see me and asked me to talk to the patient on the Burn Unit. She said I couldn't go into his room but could go as far as the door. I told her I would do it for her and as I neared the Burn Unit I could hear screams and cries from inside.

I asked Rusty what was wrong with him and she said he had been like that for two weeks and that they had taken his meds from him that morning. As I entered the Burn Unit I noticed that "my room" was empty and that the patient was in Mr. C's room. I got to his door and knocked before peeking in.

He stopped screaming when he saw me and asked if I was coming to give him back his meds. I told him I wasn't and that I had been a patient in the next room for three months. I asked why he was screaming, and he said that he didn't have any morphine, so I asked why that mattered? He told me that he needed the medication to dull the pain and asked how I had managed when I was taken off the meds. I told him that I had pretended that I had the medication and it was just as good as if I actually had it.

"Really?" he asked.

"Really", I said, "you should try it. Imagine the nurse is coming in right now and giving you the needle and then wait for a few moments for it to take effect."

It worked. Rusty told me later that he didn't shout and holler any more. She said that she went in later and told him that I had never made a sound for the three months that I was in there and I guess that must have had an effect on him as well. My good deed for the day!

One of the grafts on my shoulder didn't "take" and began to rot and smell inside the bandage. When the bandages were taken off and the area exposed it had to be cleaned and dressings were applied to heal it without further grafting. Dr. Anderson said it would scar and I laughed and said, "What's another one?"

He smiled and said, "That's true," before exiting the room, leaving the nurses to remove my stitches. There was one nurse on each side of me preparing to take them out. First I could feel the pinch, but it hurt less when I looked while they were removing the stitch and I was prepared. I asked the nurses to pull them out one at a time so I could see each one and they complied. I stopped counting at 250.

I stayed an extra week in the hospital while the dressing on my shoulder healed and when the stitches were removed from my leg I was allowed to go home. My friends came to visit now that they were studying in St. John's, so each evening while I was in the hospital, my room was full. It was a great feeling.

I went back to the hell I called Civil Engineering almost a month later, not having seen anyone from my class in that time. No teachers, no students. Losing a month was more than I could catch up with and, unlike my high school, there was no help available. I had little choice but to quit.

The next year the civil engineering program was changed to three years which meant I would have to go back for two more years. I told my parents I didn't like it enough to waste another two years on it, so I decided to stay home until I knew what I wanted to do. I was so glad to be away from that situation. However, the bad experience made me draw more into myself. I kept my burns and scars hidden so that I wouldn't stand out from the norm. Time had helped even out the colour on my face, and makeup did the rest. Even in the hottest days of summer I wore a long sleeved shirt. This was my new normal.

In May 1983 the police showed up at our house in North Harbour with a subpoena to appear in court in Placentia on June 24th, a month later.

My mother was very upset and asked the officer why he was putting her through this. He was very professional and told her that it was something that had to happen because there had been multiple deaths. She said that she wasn't going and he told her that it was an order from the court and that she could be arrested if she didn't appear. He had a subpoena for us all – Mom, Dad, Eddy, Neil, Larry and me (Mary had not been home the night of the fire so she was spared from this). Some members of the community who were first on the scene and people from the neighbouring volunteer fire department also got them. We all had to go to court.

On June 15th I had another appointment with Dr. Anderson. A strange lump had appeared underneath one of the smaller skin grafts on the back of my hand. Over time this had become infected and broken through the skin. I called it my personal volcano because when I moved my thumb back and forth the lump would move in and out of the hole in my hand. When Dr. Anderson saw it he said that the stitch must have embedded in the tendon and was trying to work its way out.

He stuck a few needles in the back of my hand to deaden the area, and covered it in green sterile cloths before cutting it open to get at the stitch. I watched as he pulled on the line and cut it off near the tendon before giving me four more stitches. My hand was bandaged for another ten days waiting for it to heal. There were no problems this time.

June 19th came and went - the third anniversary of the fire. It was always hard on the 19th; Mom didn't sleep, she stayed up all night as she had for each of the two years previous. I was the same; there was an anxious feeling in the pit of my stomach every year on that day. I couldn't control it any more than my mother could. But nobody talked about it. There was a quiet and sad silence in the house. And now the pending judicial enquiry made it that much worse.

> *"We shall draw from the heart of suffering itself*
> *the means of inspiration and survival."*
> ~ Winston Churchill

We went to Placentia as scheduled. The courthouse was a place that I had never entered and hoped never to again.

Judge G. J. Barnable conducted the enquiry. Witnesses were called: members of the volunteer fire department, and of the St. John's Regional Fire Department, the fire commissioner, the coroner, and the first police responders. My family was questioned individually, near the end.

I learned a few things that day that I had not known before, because nobody talked about them, and because I wasn't there afterwards for so many months.

Dad was the first one of the family to be questioned and I could see that it was so hard on him when he talked about being outside realizing that there was no way to get back in and not knowing who was out. He spoke about how terribly fast things had happened. There was no time to think, just to act.

Larry, Eddy and Neil each had their turn and they too found it quite difficult. So did the other people in the court. Everyone around me was crying, but not me. My heart was breaking but I would not give in.

When it was Mom's turn she asked the judge why he was doing this to her and to all of us. He told her that he understood that this was hard; it was not personal but had to be done and he would try to make it as quick as possible.

She wept as she told how she had tried to help us out and how she was getting blankets ready not realizing the door had closed or that the fire had exploded outside the room. She told about trying to get out of the room to help but having to go out the window in hopes that she could get in somewhere else if someone was inside. She cried aloud in sadness and despair as she said there was no way back in and she didn't know who was out. She cried out, "Poor Francis, poor Richard, poor Sharon, poor Harold, poor Barry are gone." She was inconsolable and had to be led from the witness box back to the chairs.

Then I had to follow my mother. I forced myself to be strong and not to cry. I would not be broken. I didn't know why that was so important; I just did not want my mother or father, or any of my family to blame themselves for my injuries. I wasn't hurt that badly.

As I approached the witness stand I looked calm and cool. I had gone through everything for them to keep them strong and I would not fail them now. The judge asked me to tell him what had happened the night of the fire and I relayed the story as I have told it here. I looked straight ahead at a place on the paneled wall above the door. I was aware of my mother's heartbreaking cries but deliberately detached myself as I spoke. The judge asked me a few questions based on the statement I had given the police officer back in September 1980. I spoke clearly and concisely as I answered.

When he was finished Judge Barnable looked at the court reporter and asked her to stop recording for a minute. She nodded and he turned to me and said that in all of his days as a judge he had never seen anyone as composed as I was under the circumstances. He said he didn't know what to make of it, whether it was a good thing or a bad thing, but that he was impressed with how I handled myself for somebody so young. He looked back at the court reporter again and nodded and then told me I was dismissed. I left the witness box walking as straight and tall as I could and sat beside my mother. She leaned into me and wept openly as I tried to console her and my father hugged her from the other side. I could taste blood from the inside of my cheeks as I continued to bite them in an effort not to cry.

It was over; we could get on with our lives.

The judicial enquiry had been called because people had died and the justice system said an investigation had to be arranged and a cause determined. People had talked and hurtful rumours had circulated without anyone realizing how hurtful they were. Rumours that Eddy had been cooking and had fallen asleep with something on the stove, or that traditional beach fires some students (including myself) had lit to celebrate the end of the school year had sparked the fire, were addressed and dismissed at the enquiry.

The enquiry concluded that there were no buttons turned to the "on" position on the electric stove, and Dad had testified that he had looked out into the kitchen and porch when he went for Mr. Jer and saw no flame or smoke. The fire in the woodstove had been out for many hours so that was ruled out. The panel box was not the culprit because of our testimony about where the fire appeared first, and the Fire Commissioner's scene investigation.

There was no determined cause. We had gone through that entire episode to establish that there was "no determined cause" for the fire. That was what the judicial enquiry would state. The devastation and loss had no determined cause, wasn't that just dandy? No determined cause.

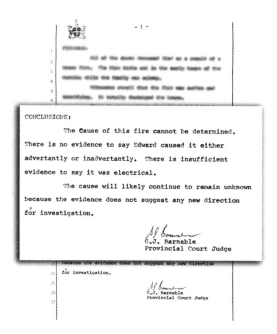

However, based on the testimony I heard that day, a few facts fell into place for me.

I didn't realize that when the police and fire department had gone in for the bodies they had thought that only four people were casualties of the fire. They were under the impression that Richard had escaped because somebody had thought they saw him outside. When the police matched up who was on the scene (which was only Eddy because he had refused to leave), and who was at the hospital (me, my parents, Neil and later Larry), they realized they had to search the site for another body. That there was confusion over who was actually home didn't help the matter.

I had met Richard in the hall that night and from where he was found later in the debris, I knew he had not made it much further than that encounter. He probably died only seconds after we ran into each other in the hall because there was no human way possible to get down those stairs.

Neil had told me that Richard was gone from the room before Larry, but I had met him after Larry had gone back to his room. Maybe he had passed out from the smoke near his own room and woke after Larry went back to their room, only to go into the hall where he got trapped. Perhaps he had been like me when I got in the closet and crouched in the fetal position, wanting to stay there. Neil also talked about how Richard had gotten up and put on his pants, shirt and sneakers very slowly and very deliberately as if he knew it was his last time. We would never know.

Sharon was also found near Richard, which meant that she must have died around the same time and only a few steps from me where I lost her. She may have become entangled with Richard when I got knocked off the stair rail, which was why I couldn't find her, or she may have thought he was me.

Francis, Harold and Barry were found in what would have been their bedroom. I doubt that they ever woke that morning although Mom thought she heard Barry say he couldn't see. She later said she wasn't sure that she had heard anyone and I figured, if she did, maybe it had been Richard.

All five had died from smoke inhalation, which was a relief in a strange sort of way; it meant they wouldn't have suffered as much as dying from the flames.

A year or so later we learned that a particular brand of clothes dryer had been recalled because they were deemed a fire hazard and a cause of early morning fire-related deaths. These dryers had live wires in a constant "on" state, and were known to short out, causing a fire. The laundry room was attached to the house in the porch underneath our bedroom window. The door to the laundry room was always closed and the roof of the porch had been on fire from underneath while the porch itself was clear for Eddy to get out through that morning. The laundry room would also have been attached to the boys' room causing that bedroom to smoke up before any of the rest.

We were never sure that we had owned the particular brand of dryer that was reported as a fire hazard; however, it made the most sense and we took it as an answer when we had none. And that was important.

My arm was not getting the mobility it should because the skin was so tight on my back and arm. When I visited Dr. Anderson in January he said that he would try one more time to alleviate the tightness caused by the scarring. In February, 1984 I was brought in for my last surgery.

This time the skin grafting was going to be harvested in a new way. Dr. Anderson explained that he would cut the skin going down my back near where my arm was connected. He would make a sort of flap there and then cut the skin going down the inside of my arm and insert the flap of skin, which, when it healed would allow me to move my right arm up over my head. I was willing to try.

He also said I needed to have the tension released in several places in both arms and that the skin would come from the inside of my right arm. He would make a shallow cut on the top layer of skin, harvest the next few layers of skin underneath and then stitch the top layer over that. He told me that this way I would not need to stay in the hospital.

I had surgery on Thursday morning and when I woke up both my arms were bandaged and snugly wrapped in slings in front of my body. Dr. Anderson was there and told me I could go home and to keep my arms in the slings for the next two weeks before coming back to see him.

I was helpless again. I needed somebody to help me with the bathroom, feed me, dress me and attend to my needs for the next two weeks. I had become so independent over the last couple of years it was like taking a step back. However, according to the doctor, it was for the best.

When I got back to North Harbour I was in my comfort zone again. Everyone was so nice to me, coming to visit, bringing me gifts, keeping me company. North Harbour was a place of calm within all my storms and I so appreciated every minute I spent there as I healed. All the people looked after me as if I were their own.

After a couple of days getting over the anesthetic I was able to get out around and go to the Shop to spend time with people and to visit the graves again. I found comfort most of all when I visited the graves. Although everyone was good to me I still had something missing.

To the outside world I was surrounded by people, smiling and happy, but I felt alone and sad. It was hard to explain. Nobody could walk a mile in my shoes, nobody understood me and some of that was because nobody close to the events of that horrible night ever talked about anything, including me. I didn't want to cause anyone pain by bringing it up.

Every year on June 19th the community came together to remember the loss. To outsiders, we were "the family with the fire." It was what defined us. I was "a victim of a horrible tragedy." And that defined me. I had to come to terms with that, and to live with it.

On February 29th, 1984 I got the one hundred or so stitches out of the skin grafts on my arms and could ditch the slings forever. On March 7th I had the forty stitches out of the donor site. I walked out of the hospital for the last time as a burn patient – almost four years after the fire.

I was free physically, but not psychologically. I remained covered to the world, so I would not have to talk about what happened, and to avoid stares from those who would not understand. I guess I wasn't really free.

*"Your heart has been sore wounded too. Dear Light,
love shall cherish you, till you again look on life with happy eyes."*
~ Byron Caldwell Smith, letter to Kate Stephens

During the summer of 1984 I met the man I would marry – Thomas Young. He was so kind and caring and he taught me how to laugh. As we got to know each other I asked him what he thought about my scars, but all he would say was that I was beautiful. He told me he only saw my strength, that he never saw my scars. We were married on a rainy Saturday in October, 1986. We had no money to speak of so I borrowed a wedding dress and we both had plain gold bands. It was not extravagant but we were happy.

Our first Christmas together, he had given me a beautiful short-sleeved green dress and I asked him why when he knew I only wore things with long sleeves. He said that it would look great on me, but I refused to wear it and asked him to take it back. I told him I didn't want anyone to look at my burns. Despite his coaxing I would not give in. I had control over that part of my life and it was one thing I would not compromise on. I didn't mind telling people what happened to me because I could be selective of who I told and what I told. But I didn't want anyone looking at me, wondering what happened, how it happened, and asking me about it. I stayed covered up.

I was working at a minimum wage job in St. John's before we were married, but I followed my husband to St. Bride's where he worked in the fish plant, and I could get a job there. I liked life in the small communities as it was less complicated. The people of St. Bride's welcomed me and I made some great friends. St. John's had not been good to me; it reminded me of all my surgeries, my attempts at high school and college. These were not good memories.

We lived in Thomas' grandfather's old house and started to save every cent we made at the fish plant to build a home.

I couldn't wait to have children of my own, to love uncondition-
ally, who would fill up my days and who could accept me for who
I was. With all my body had been through over the past several
years it wasn't until January, 1990 that I had a baby girl. I named
her Sharon. I had wanted so badly to give my beloved sister a
namesake.

With the fishing industry fading away, our finances dwindled.
Life was difficult, but it was so good to have my baby girl. Thomas
and I had had barely enough work to get Employment Insurance,
and what little we had we put it into our house. It was only partially finished but it had plumbing and was warm – the necessities.
It was a hard existence but I had learned that life was hard and I
could cope with hard as long as I was loved.

Almost two months after bringing Sharon home she got terribly sick and ended up in the hospital. When I faced that crisis I
realized what my mother must have gone through when she was
helpless the night of the fire. Thankfully, Sharon got better. The
next year I had another baby girl, Stacey, and, two years later,
Shawna. Our family was complete.

But our meager existence had worsened over those few years
and things were slowly going downhill. The fishery had com-
pletely shut down the year before and both myself and Thomas
were jobless.

Sharon was four, Stacey was two, Shawna was born in October of 1993, Thomas was receiving income from what was referred
to as TAGS, getting $402 every two weeks, and I had no other
income. (TAGS was The Atlantic Groundfish Strategy income
replacement program put in place by the Federal Department of
Fisheries for displaced fishery workers. The amount a person received was prorated according to the amount they earned from
the fishery, either on a boat or in a fish plant.)

Shawna was in the Janeway for a few weeks in November, in
critical care with a severe lung infection, and this took a major

toll on us as a family – first emotionally, but also physically and especially financially. It was a terrible time. Her pediatrician let her go a little early so I could rest and "get well" myself as I had complications after her birth, and we could get home as a family with it being so close to Christmas. There was one condition: I had to take Shawna back to the hospital the following week for a follow-up. I think he pitied me because I felt and must have looked terrible.

The next week, we decided to take the other two girls along to see Santa, and Neil offered to drive our car. Since the girls never got to go to St. John's at all this would be a treat for them, and we had to go anyway. On the way out to the hospital we were in a car accident on the slippery road. The rear-view mirror came off the windshield and flew into the back, hitting the seat and then hitting Shawna in the head as she faced the rear in her car seat. She howled.

A passing driver stopped and brought us to a clinic, but when we got there it was closed. Neil had someone bring his car to the clinic to drive us to the Janeway. On the way Shawna went silent – from howling to horribly silent. Neil kept asking how she was and I told him she was fine even though I thought she was dead. I wouldn't dare say anything, I just held her tight, hoping against hope that I was wrong, but sure that I was right.

When we got to the hospital I walked in still holding her and I stretched out my arms and said, "We were in a car accident and I don't know if she is dead or alive." The nurse took her from me immediately and rushed into a room with me close behind her, now in tears. Shortly after, Shawna finally made a sound. She was kept there all day but thankfully was fine, although they were worried about a brain bleed.

Neil and his wife, Trudy, took the other two girls to the Avalon Mall to see Santa and then came back for us when Shawna was discharged. On the way back to North Harbour we passed the accident scene and realized the car – an old beater, but a lifeline – was a total loss and we were all lucky to be alive.

With all the turmoil, Christmas crept up on us really quickly that year. It was very stressful just wondering how we were going to get through the month, let alone worry about Christmas. I spent a lot of time worrying and crying to myself, because as a mother I should be able to provide good things for my children, and this year I knew it wouldn't happen. It was breaking my heart to know that they would be disappointed so young and that there wasn't one thing I could do about it. Their life was becoming hard and that killed me because I didn't want them to have hardship like I did, like my mother did.

Sharon looked through the Sears Christmas catalogue and her eyes would light up at all the toys displayed on the pages. Her friends were all excited and talking about what they were going to get from Santa, and she was wondering what he was going to bring her but she never asked for anything. Stacey was excited too and they both couldn't wait for Santa to come, because they had been so good all year and were being extra good since Shawna was brought home from the hospital. I was so proud of them, which hurt even more because there would be no reward for their being good.

It was December 15th and Thomas was expecting his last TAGS cheque before Christmas. We had decided that we would spend that $402 on the girls and on food and would leave the bills to be paid sometime after Christmas. We hoped that it wouldn't take much to put some big stuffed animals and toys under the tree to at least make it look like the girls had lots of stuff.

I wanted a turkey because Christmas just wasn't the same without one. We decided to splurge on that and cut back in other areas of the grocery list just to bring some normalcy to Christmas Day.

Thomas went to the mail and there was no cheque. The same thing happened the next two days. Here it was the weekend before

Christmas and we had nothing, and I mean nothing for Christmas – no food, no gifts and any hope I had left was fading away. Things were hard in so many ways that were beyond our control and I wondered if that was going to be our lot in life. I didn't know how much more I could take.

Yet, this was to be the best Christmas I could ever imagine, when the true meaning of Christmas was revealed to me in the kindness and good deeds of others. And this in turn brought me to the realization that, for my girls' sake, I could not continue in this way. I might be a victim of this life but there was no reason for the cycle to continue for them.

That weekend, my parents, along with Neil and his wife and kids, dropped by from North Harbour and put some things under the tree for the girls from all of them. They brought two home-made cakes and the makings of another one to get the "smell of Christmas" in the house, which my mother proceeded to do once she got settled.

Thomas' parents and family had gifts for the girls at their house for Christmas morning, as was their tradition, so I knew the girls would be happy with that. They invited us for Christmas dinner; however, I wanted to spend it at home if possible. Although they all knew we were struggling, nobody knew how dire our situation was because we didn't want them to worry.

Monday came and still no cheque. "Despair" doesn't do justice to what we were feeling. We made phone calls about the cheque and found that a lot of people hadn't gotten theirs and that a mail-bag may have been misrouted because of the extra mail that comes with the season. It was now only three days to Christmas Eve.

I was sitting in the living room feeding Shawna when my friend, a teacher, came to wish us a Merry Christmas. She was going home for the Holidays and wanted to drop in for a few minutes to see me before she left. She couldn't stay and left in a hurry. A few minutes later another friend dropped by because she, too, was going home for Christmas. She had a little gift bag for me and said to open it later that day when I had a chance and not to leave it until Christmas. I felt bad that I had nothing for her and she said that I had been her friend in difficult times, and that she was grateful for the many cups of tea we shared, and that had been my gift to her.

Thomas burst through the door a short time later and I could see by the smile and look of relief that the cheque had finally come. Although people say that money isn't everything, being without it sure is a torture. We made arrangements for somebody to babysit and planned to hire a car to take us to get groceries and some gifts for Christmas morning.

Since the accident, we didn't have a car and the closest place for shopping was in Placentia, about a forty-five minute drive. Thomas' brother wasn't using his truck that day and offered it to us. The cost of hiring a car would have eaten into our budget, so this was great news.

While we were waiting on the babysitter, Thomas asked me about a card on top of the fridge. I didn't know what he was talking about so he brought it to me. I opened the card and started to cry. My teacher friend had left a $50 bill in a card for me to find when she was gone. I realized that was why she had left so quickly.

It then struck me that my other friend had told me to look in the gift bag she had brought. I went over to the tree and opened the bag. There was a little gift pack for me and an envelope with a $100 grocery gift certificate. I started to cry again because these friends had helped relieve some of the tremendous pressure that we were under that Christmas.

Sharon and Stacey ran to me and hugged into my legs asking what was wrong. I told them Mommy was having a happy cry not a sad cry. This made me cry even more. Then I thought of my mother telling me about one Christmas long ago when Marg had given her $10. She and Dad had had nothing at all and it had saved her. That was a lot of money in the early 1960s. I was a wreck and had to pull myself together just to get out of the house.

In Placentia we got everything we had on our list, though we had managed to underestimate the cost. We bought some nice Santa cookies and some Christmas candy too. Most of the shelves at the bargain store were bare, as most of the toys had been picked through, but we bought a few extra things for the girls because we knew they were little and didn't really care that something was expensive, just that they had "stuff" on Christmas morning. When we got home that evening and paid the babysitter, most of our money was gone but we were proud of what we had managed on our tight budget with the extra boost from our friends.

The next evening I heard a knock at the door. There was a girl with two cans of formula and a small gift for each of the girls. She said that I had given her mom two cans of milk for her baby sister back in October when she had needed it and that had saved her mom a lot of trouble. Her mom was now returning the milk and wanted to give me something for the three girls. I couldn't speak and gave her a hug and when she left I started to cry again. Thomas asked me what was wrong and I couldn't tell him because I didn't know. People were being so nice and that meant a lot when I was so down, feeling stressed and possibly had the "baby blues."

The kids were being extra good and were very excited about Santa. I went to Christmas Eve Mass at 9pm while Thomas stayed home and got the kids ready for bed. The church was all lit for Christmas and everyone was happy and bustling and I thought it wasn't such a bad Christmas after all. I had a lot to be thankful for. Shawna, so near death only a few weeks before, was now thriving, and the other two girls were so precious to me. Life wasn't without its troubles but it was what it was and I thanked God for that.

When I got home the house was quiet. Thomas met me just inside the door and he held his fingers to his lips for me not to make a sound. I thought the kids were probably asleep in the living room but when I went further and could see the lights of the Christmas tree I couldn't believe my eyes.

I didn't understand how there were so many gifts and toys under the tree that weren't there before I went to Mass. He said Eddy had gotten in from Toronto that evening to spend Christmas with my parents. He had picked up Mom and came to our house to drop off some things from Santa. I couldn't believe it; there must have been ten or twelve extra things for each of the girls. They would be so happy when they saw the pages of the Sears catalogue come to life under the tree.

I was overwhelmed. This was what Christmas was about. Not the things that were under the tree but the feeling that I had in my heart right at that moment. I couldn't cry any more, I just looked at the tree knowing I had three beautiful healthy daughters who would have a joyous Christmas, and I felt that everything was right with the world for a change. Life was only hard if I looked for the hard things. I didn't think Christmas could get any better – but it wasn't over yet.

The next day I was proud to have a turkey cooking, thanks to my friends. The kids were excited and couldn't stop talking, and jumping, and laughing, and every "happy" thing you could think of. The phone was ringing with "Season's Greetings" from family and friends. I put the stresses of catching up on bills after Christmas out of my mind and decided to enjoy the day as it was meant to be. We visited Thomas' parents and the girls got gifts and stockings there, then we returned home to tend to the meal.

We had Christmas dinner around 1pm and while we were sitting down a knock came on the door. Before I could get out to see who it was, our neighbour came in shouting "Ho, Ho, Ho." The girls ran to him giving him hugs and kisses and shouting all at once about what Santa had brought them.

Our neighbour carried a huge Christmas gift bag, almost waist high. After greeting the kids and seeing their toys, he gave me the gift bag and said it was a little something for the girls from him and his wife. I reached for the bag and tears filled my eyes as I gave him a big hug. I invited him to stay but he shook hands with Thomas and wished us all a Merry Christmas and left. When I looked in the bag there were many boxes of different types of chocolates, expensive candies, large bags of chips, cards for each of the girls, little toys, syrup and drinks and a whole bundle of nice things to eat that I had not been able to get when we were shopping. I remembered passing some of the things at the pharmacy and saying how great it would be to have the "nice chocolates" – short for expensive chocolates – instead of the package of dollar ones I had bought. This was our wish list of nice things to have around for when people dropped by, and so much more. Christmas was complete. For the second time in two days, I was overwhelmed!

I thought of the cartoon *How the Grinch Stole Christmas* that we had watched a few days before and how the Grinch's heart had had grown three sizes. That was mine today. I had felt as dismal and desperate as the Grinch only the day before. Although it was the worst of circumstances, I will never forget that Christmas, and I swore that day that sometime my circumstances would change, and I would be the person who helped make somebody else feel the way I felt at that moment. I also swore that my life was going to change; it would not always be a struggle. I was determined to get my girls out of that existence of poverty and stress as soon as I got the opportunity, and I would make an opportunity if one could not be found.

TAGS required that Thomas had to go to school. He went to St. John's from Monday to Friday for a nine-month course in bricklaying. He didn't want to be in the city and found it really difficult to be away with the kids so small, but he would lose the funding if he quit. That $402 every two weeks was barely enough to keep us going but there was really nothing else.

Once Thomas was finished school things became even more difficult financially because I could not get any work, and Thomas didn't want to go bricklaying with no jobs close to home. There was talk that Argentia would get a big project related to the oil or mining, so I said this was my chance to be ready for opportunities that were sure to be there. I told Thomas that I was going to look into attending school too, that we had to do something.

At this time my father was diagnosed with an advanced form of prostate cancer. He tried chemo and radiation before being put on pills and sent home. That was hard on all of us, but especially my mother. They were both living at home by themselves now, although Neil built a place next door to them a few years later.

Thomas was very supportive of my going back to school and told me to look into getting federal government funding through the Employment Program. There was very little help available because most of the federal funds went into the TAGS program. A lot of private training programs had popped up since the fishery closed and it was even harder to get into school.

I went to a meeting in July and discovered that there were only going to be two students sponsored in Placentia and St. Mary's Bays combined. There were more than fifty people at this meeting and more were scheduled for other places. It was a long-shot but I was going to go for it. Poverty was not a condition I wanted to stay in because it was plain and simply too hard.

I met with a counsellor in August who was trying to determine how serious clients were about going to school. We talked for a little while and I told her I was interested in doing something in the computer industry – that I wanted to be employable when the big projects came to the Placentia area. She told me to contact the College of Trades and Technology in St. John's, because there were no computer programs offered in the local area.

I called the phone number she had given me and a man on the other end said, "What do you want?" I laughed nervously saying that I was interested in doing a computer program and was wondering if there were any openings.

He asked me if I was a "MacGyver" or a "secretary" and I said a "MacGyver." (*MacGyver* was a TV drama where the star could get out of any situation by using common objects around him so I knew he was asking if I minded getting my hands dirty or working with my hands.) He told me there was one seat left in the Computer Support Program and that he would put my name on it if I wanted. I said yes but told him that I couldn't go if I wasn't funded. He said this was a very new program and there was lots of interest in it so he would have no trouble filling the seat if I couldn't make it.

I didn't know this at the time but this man was not supposed to be in the office for another week. He had gone in that day for an hour and answered my call just before leaving. If he had not been there my opportunity would have been lost. Something was pointing me in a new direction – the stars were aligning.

I called the counsellor and told her that I had a seat at the College if I was accepted for funding at 80% of the total cost of the program. She said she would get back to me the next day, which she did, with good news – she said I was accepted and that I had to report to school on Tuesday. I asked, "What Tuesday?" and she said, "Next week."

So now I was in trouble. I felt like a cat chasing a mouse – now that I had it, what would I do with it? I had to be in school the next week; I had no money and nowhere to stay. Sharon was going to Grade 1, Stacey was starting Kindergarten and Shawna would soon be three. But I was going to make it work. I had to, it was as much or more for them than it was for me.

Thomas was glad for me because he knew how much I wanted this and he said that I was going, and there was no more to it than that. He was so supportive. I called Mary, who lived close to the college, and she said I could stay with her and her son Scott. And so began our journey out of poverty.

Like Thomas had, I stayed in St. John's during the week and could only get home on the weekends. Unlike Thomas, my course would take two and half years to complete, a long time away from small children. This was going to be a sacrifice but I was going to make it worth it.

The school work came easy for me. I caught on to new concepts fairly quickly and time flew by. Every evening during the week I would stay after school, especially during exams, and help several of my classmates. We studied together and I worked hard.

The weekends went too fast and I looked forward to the ones with a holiday Monday, to have an extra day to spend more time with the girls. Thomas was doing a fantastic job at home with them but I knew it was hard for him too so the long weekends were great for him as well. I had been by myself when he was in school and I knew how challenging it could be.

Every weekend we tried to spend a day visiting my mother and father. I wanted to try to assure them that we were all doing fine and to keep them company as I knew they were longing for somebody to be around. Dad's treatment was discontinued while I was in the middle of exams. That was very difficult to hear and made our visits all the more special.

Each Monday it was getting harder and harder to leave home. I cried on Sundays and Thomas always told me to go and not be a quitter. He had faith in me, which gave me a renewed energy and faith in myself.

Even though she would be asleep, Stacey wanted to know that I kissed her before I left so I always put on lipstick on Monday mornings and kissed her cheek, leaving the lipstick for her to find. Sharon was thriving in school and was fine with me being gone as long as I brought her something every Friday. Thomas had started that tradition when he went to school the year before so I had to continue it. Shawna was so young that I was afraid she would forget me and one particular weekend at home was nearly my undoing.

She had been to the school one day that week when her dad had gone to parent-teacher night. She drew a picture of our family and proudly ran to me on Friday evening showing off her drawing. It was a picture of an island with a palm tree in the middle, surrounded by blue crayon scribbled water, and on the island were three small stick figures and one bigger one. I smiled as I looked at the picture and she proudly told me it was her family. She said, "This is me, and this is Sta, and this is Sharry, and this is Daddy. Do you like our family Mommy?" Then she looked down at the picture and I could just barely hold back the tears.

She looked up at me with her huge brown eyes and a big gap toothed smile and I smiled back at her although I was dying inside. I laid my hand on her smiling face and I said to myself right then that I was staying home, there was no way I was letting my children forget me no matter how much I wanted a better life for them. She looked down at the drawing, and looked at me, then down at the paper. When she looked up again her eyes widened even more and she said, "Right there behind that tree is you, Mommy!" and she proceeded to draw a head sticking out from behind the palm tree. She was so happy that she drew our family. I lifted her up and held her tight and told her I loved her. Thomas hugged us both and told Shawna it was an amazing picture. He said she must be an artist, she was so smart. That weekend I almost didn't go back but Thomas pleaded with me not to give up.

When the girls were out of school for both summers, I brought them into St. John's with me and put them in day camp while Thomas went fishing with his uncle for the summer. The scaled back fishery had opened by this time. The girls had a wonderful time and we did a lot of things together before they went back to St. Bride's for school again when the summers were over. It didn't make it any easier to leave them again but I only had one semester of school left and an unpaid work term that was planned for Placentia in the winter. After almost two years I could commute from home.

Christmas couldn't come soon enough; I could finally stop the "weekend mom" deal and get back to something normal. I was looking forward to that. When December came and finals were over I said goodbye to my classmates and headed home. Home to my family! I would graduate in April after the work term and would see my school friends again at that time.

Between Christmas and New Year I got a call from the college. It was bad news. There was a strike at the site of my work term and I would not be allowed to go there to finish my course. If I didn't do the work term, I wouldn't graduate. So I had to head back to St. John's for fourteen more weeks. I was disappointed, to say the least; however I had to do it. After almost two years going back and for in another few weeks it would be over – if I looked at it like that it was bearable.

I called Mary again and told her what happened and she told me to come on back with her until I was finished. I packed up all my belongings that I had unpacked when I got home and headed off for the Federal Department of Fisheries and Oceans (DFO). The time flew by there and I loved the work. It was great; I learned a lot and gained confidence and experience.

As April approached there was no sign of any industry coming to Placentia and myself and Thomas talked about our options. He told me that I wasn't coming home after spending over two years in school, even if it meant going away to the mainland to get more experience I would have to do that. It was no point sacrificing for the last couple of years only to come home and be in the same position we were in before I left. He was right, as much as I didn't want to admit it. Fortunately I didn't have to make that decision as I was offered a six month contract at DFO. I was still away from the girls but it meant experience for me.

Graduation in April was a grand affair. Thomas was fishing and I knew he couldn't come in to see me walk across the stage. But as a surprise he showed up with the three girls. I was so happy. I was awarded the President's Medal for the highest overall marks in the computer course that I just finished and the Governor General Medal of Honor for having the highest marks in the province in any post-secondary field. Normally there were seven Governor General Medals given out for each college sector but that year the college system had been remodeled and only one medal was awarded. I also received a $2000 scholarship, which was truly amazing. I had worked hard, and been through a lot and was now rewarded for it. Looking back I could barely understand how I had managed to get through it but I had.

I only told a few close friends at college about the tragedy our family had endured and I was always careful to keep myself in long sleeved tops to cover my scars. No matter what I did, I was always cognizant of my burns. I would never say nor ever thought it was a barrier but it was something that was a constant in my life: the unspeakable tragedy and the lifetime of hurt.

The girls spent the summer with me again attending camps in St. John's and then I had to let them go back to St. Bride's to go back to school. I wrote three exams that fall for federal jobs and was lucky to get a placement and later a permanent position after a successful competition. That also meant we had to make a choice. We both wanted us all to be together so it was either I continued to be a long distance mother or we had to move out of St. Bride's. The second option seemed like the best.

We bought a house, which was such a foreign concept. I had paid more in taxes that year at work then I had ever made annually in my life. When the girls finished their school year in St. Bride's they moved in and when Thomas finished fishing that summer he joined us in our new home. Change was the norm now. New neighbours, new friends. I thought of the girls switching to a large new school from their old one in St. Bride's and it brought me nightmares, and flashbacks of my experience at Holy Heart years ago. I would have to be sure that they didn't go through what I had. Life seemed to always be mired in turmoil or stress.

In February the next year, 2001, my father lost his battle with cancer – almost a decade after being sent home to die. He never talked about the fire but before he died I asked him some questions about what he saw and how he felt that night and I have included those details in this story. He was very saddened by his loss but knew he had to go on for the sake of the rest of his family. He never gave up his faith in God and tried to pass it on to us just how important it was. He went to the church every day that I could remember, unless he physically could not get there. When that happened he always said an extra rosary.

Dad loved the outdoors. I never knew him to ever say a bad word against any person. He was always kind and gracious. He died in the winter of the biggest snowfall on record in Newfoundland in over a hundred years. There were storms every day that year except for each day that he was waked, when the sun shone and the sky was clear.

The first morning of his wake I went to the church by myself at 6am to spend some time with my dad. Although I had experienced great loss in my life I had never publicly grieved and I wanted to spend these morning hours privately grieving this man who had shaped my life. I talked to him, sometimes out loud and sometimes from my head. I told him how glad I was to have him as a father and how much of an influence he had on my life. When

I asked him if he was listening and if he was with his children, a solitary petal from one of the roses on his casket fell at my feet, and I took this to mean that he heard and he was.

After burying my father, my mother was alone. She said you are meant to go through life with a partner and she didn't want to spend a night by herself, so that is how it was. She took up primary residence with Mary but spent many months with her sister May, or with either me or my brothers and our families.

Although she had been through tougher times than any single person should have to deal with, she always had a smile, even though her heart was broken underneath. I had learned that from her, too – put on a good face on the outside and hide what is on the inside. It is easier.

Part 3

"It has been said, 'time heals all wounds.' I do not agree.
The wounds remain. In time, the mind, protecting its sanity,
covers them with scar tissue and the pain lessens. But it is never gone."
~ Rose Kennedy

We settled into life in our new home, our children made great friends and loved the "new life" offered outside of their St. Bride's home. We were finally together as a family, and life became fast-paced with things such as bringing kids to sports and volunteering as a coach or helper.

I thought I was happy and I was because I wasn't sad. And I lived life as I thought it was meant to be lived – as a burned person hiding under clothing. I had no further expectation for myself.

Several years later, while watching TV, I saw an advertisement looking for children to attend an Atlantic Burn Camp in Nova Scotia. I thought to myself that maybe I could help out in Newfoundland and Labrador in some way since I certainly had experience in the burn part of burn camp.

Me and my big ideas!

I procrastinated for a while, but in 2007 I made the call, left a message somewhere in New Brunswick, as indicated on the commercial, and the next day I got a call from a person in Gander, NL. The network for the camp was extensive. "Hi Ida," this gentleman said, "I understand you want to volunteer with the Atlantic Burn Camp (ABC), can you tell me why you are interested?"

I told him that I liked to volunteer my time to charitable organizations and that I had been thinking about the ABC for a few years. I told him that I had been burned when I was fifteen and that I would have liked to have the opportunity to attend a burn camp at that time, so I just thought I would help out if there was a need.

He asked me what I thought I could do for the camp and I mentioned that I could help with anything that needed organizing during the year or could be a resource in my area. He said, "Why don't you come along to camp, you never know but you might get something more out of it than the kids."

I asked if I was allowed to go, and he assured me it was perfectly fine so, without thinking, I said yes. The camp was in less than a month, and I had to make sure I could get it off from work, but as easy as that – I was going to camp. As I waved goodbye to Thomas and my three girls the next month I had no idea what I was in for.

I drove the ten hours across the Island, picked up two counsellors along the way, and met up with two others, including some campers, in Stephenville before proceeding to the Port aux Basques ferry. After the eight-hour ferry crossing, our group was picked up on the Nova Scotia dock by Burn Camp volunteers who brought us to the camp location where we had breakfast with the rest of the kids and counsellors.

My day was very emotional for some reason and was very busy. I couldn't explain what I was feeling but as the day progressed I didn't like it. I was in an unfamiliar and uncomfortable place in my head and in my heart. As I stood holding hands with strangers in a huge circle of kids and adults I was overwhelmed with sadness and the urge to run. I kept silent as the group sang their song and started to circle to the right, around under the cover of the tent. I was on autopilot.

My mind was racing: how was I going to control the situation? People would think there was something wrong with me. If I could only get away! I tried to occupy my mind with something other than the situation until the song ended and then I would be alright. My jaw was clenched tight trying to hold my emotions, a lump was forming in my throat but I had to be strong. I had no reason not to be. A pain started at the pit of my stomach expanded up through my chest. *Ida get hold of yourself!*

Life had finally started to calm down and get a bit easier and now here I was in the middle of what should have been a great experience, feeling more turmoil than I had in years.

The song seemed to go on forever; then the group started to collapse the circle towards the center while holding their joined hands over their heads. I followed suit because the people on both sides of me holding my hands were doing it. "We all shine like stars, cause that's what we are," vibrated through the huge tent as kids and adults alike were shouting out the chorus to the Camp's theme song.

Finally it was over. I held still as the raised hands were dropped and people let go of each other. The children chattered with excitement and the counsellors smiled in welcome. The man on my right, that had just let go of my hand, stepped back where it was dimmer and wiped a tear from his eye – that was my undoing. I made a beeline for the exit in the white canvas tent enclosure to escape to the privacy of the bunkhouse. Nobody would be there now. *I'm tired after the long drive to Cape Breton. That's all, I'm tired.*

I don't know how I got there but I made it to the sleeping quarters at the top of the stairs in the church that served as an indoor recreation area and sleeping quarters for the campers. ABC was held for a week each year at a bible camp at the base of Kelly's Mountain. It was truly beautiful here but I was not enjoying it, I had a bad feeling about this. Surely by tomorrow I would be OK. I had claimed the bottom bunk just inside the door when we had arrived a few hours earlier and there were five more sets of bunk beds along the walls inside the blue coloured room. The room, luckily, was empty now, but would fill up later as the rest of the female counsellors and helpers – the ones not assigned to the children's bunkhouses – would be going to bed.

If I could only get to sleep before the rest of the adults returned. I turned out the battery powered lantern and squirmed into the sleeping bag, turning my head into the pillow. Tears flowed freely as the pain rising up in my chest exploded with exhaustive force and I lay there trying to get rid of this feeling and trying to sleep. I had to figure out what was wrong me.

I was tired. Tomorrow would be better, I was sure of it. I just had to get whatever this overwhelming feeling was out of my system before the next day. Maybe this crying would help get rid of it. This was unfamiliar to me and I did not like it one little bit. I was strong and I never cried!

The next morning the bell tolled somewhere out in the camp area signalling that breakfast was ready. There was a flurry of activity below the room where the bathroom showers started up. I got untangled from the sleeping bag and remembered where I was. I felt, like I am sure I looked, horrible. I was not going to cry today. As all the other counsellors in the room began to unwind from their cocoons, I gathered my clothes and headed for the shower.

All of us had gotten an ABC T-shirt and hat when our group arrived the morning before and I had pulled the T-shirt on over my long-sleeved top. I brought it down with me to put on over the next long-sleeved shirt that I had packed. It had been over twenty-seven years since I had worn anything outside in public that did not have long sleeves and I was not going to start now. I was not brave enough and I believed there were lots of medical reasons dealing with UV rays and others why I shouldn't. I was just not brave enough!

The day before, I had watched the children play and laugh; so carefree in their tanks and bathing suits. I envied them their ability to be real and suddenly I felt so fake. I had bought a bathing suit for camp; however I had no intention of wearing it, it was an impulse buy. The tags were still attached. I had wandered around the camp, not really allowing myself to be part of the program and watching from a distance as the kids laughed and giggled. I couldn't get too close to the action because my emotions were bubbling to the surface.

It would not be like that today. I would not allow it. I would try to become more involved. I came here as a volunteer but so far had proved a dud. Today would be better.

As I made my way into the main dining hall I was welcomed by the ladies in the kitchen, who were so friendly. They had my special meal prepared, mindful that I could not eat any regular breads like everyone else. (A few years prior I had been diagnosed with a severe form of Celiac Disease (gluten allergy) and had to adjust my whole eating routine around it.) The camp was very accommodating; everyone was so nice; it was like a big happy family here.

I picked up my meal and moved to join some of the counsellors and children who had come in and sat at one of the several lines of tables in the room. Everything was so organized; the tables were set with paper cups and flatware in neat rows as if somebody had taken the time to place their best china. More campers and their counsellors came in and sat all around me at the tables. They were so happy to be there. I could feel myself getting sad again and I had to try and hurry through the meal so I could get out of there. Something big was going on within me and I didn't know what it was nor could I explain it.

I finished as quickly as I could and walked up the beaten path through the grass on my way back to the room to fix up the sleeping bag and tidy the area. At least that was the excuse I gave myself as some of the stragglers skipped past on their way to breakfast, sounding off a "good morning" to me.

When I got to the room some of the counsellors were still inside drying their hair and preparing for games scheduled that day. I smiled, but as I turned to the bunk to clean up, a wayward tear escaped from the corner of my eye. I couldn't stay there because I didn't want anyone to see me. So I quickly finished what I was doing and left the building, walking out the path towards the dirt road. Surely I would be alone there and, with the exception of one runner, I was.

I walked for miles and the tears streamed down my face as I sobbed uncontrollably. I had no reason to cry, I didn't know why I was crying and that alone was making me worse. As a scattered vehicle passed by I gazed out at the lake pretending there was something of interest so the driver would not see a crazy woman crying her eyes out. The film of tears distorted everything around me and I stumbled several times over the loose rocks.

I walked for what must have been an hour before turning around and going back to the camp. I had to get hold of my emotions or I would have to go home. The internal conflict between trying to be strong, yet believing I was so weak, was exhausting. I stopped for a while on the dock below the camp to compose myself and to allow some time for the redness to leave my eyes.

It was close to lunchtime when I got back and there were water sport activities planned for that afternoon. The kids were so happy, especially the teenagers, and I imagined myself being one of them twenty-seven years before and how maybe my life would have been different if I had had others "like me." But there was no turning back, not now. Nothing could be undone and I knew that.

I managed to get through lunch but I was excluding myself from the party atmosphere. All the volunteers and kids were having such a great time and I couldn't allow myself to be in the picture. The feeling in my stomach and chest was ready to explode again and I had to get out of there once more. Off I went again, and as I walked up the road the unstoppable tears came and I could hear the echoes of the children and adults as the "water Olympics" got underway. What was I going to do? What, indeed, was I going to do?

I had talked to Thomas and the girls for a few minutes the night before and told them everything was fine. Thomas knew from my voice that it wasn't but he didn't say anything. When I was a long way away from the camp, I sat on a rock near the beach and took out my cell phone. I knew Thomas had no work today and maybe talking to him would make things much better.

When Thomas answered the phone I was crying so hard I couldn't speak. He knew it was me and, once I assured him, between heaving sobs, that it was nothing serious, he stayed quietly on the other end of the line until I was ready to talk. When I calmed enough, I managed to tell him that I was absolutely miserable. He said that it was so unlike me, that I loved working with kids. I volunteered a great deal of my time around kids, I coached softball and baseball, I helped out in the school at basketball, volleyball and any other time I was needed. I said it wasn't even that, I wanted to enjoy it, it should be something that I would enjoy, however something had gone wrong that I was unable to explain.

I talked to him until I felt better and said maybe that was all I needed to do, just talk it out although I didn't know what "it" was. I told him I was heading back from wherever I was and that I thought I would be OK for sure. I said that I would have to come home early if I didn't get myself under control.

Heading back, my mind began to clear and my emotions steadied. I was good. As I neared the camp I could see the children playing and running so carefree. I made a smile and forced it to stay on my face as I walked into the middle of the frenzy. I made it through supper but the sadness was back, I could not get rid of it. I talked silently to myself, I got mad with myself, I tried everything I could think of but the feeling would not go away.

It was time again for the camp song in the huge tent. This was a nightly ritual and had been for many years according to the long-time campers. They loved it. We all went out to the tent as one of the kids tugged vigorously on the rope attached to the bell, signalling the evening festivities. I had such a feeling of dread that I didn't want to go and I almost didn't but I kept telling myself to go – that it would be alright if I gave it a chance.

Everyone joined hands and a small child of eight or nine came and grabbed hold of me on one side and another counsellor held my hand on the other. As the music played my lips moved to the song, but no words could come out. If the words escaped so would the anguish, the despair and the tears. I had to hold on for a few minutes until it was over. I hoped the dim light hid the tortured look I was sure was on my face.

"We all shine like stars, cause that's what we are," was repeated several times, louder and louder as the song came to an end. The kids were getting reacquainted with each other, so the festivities took on an even more boisterous tone. I waited as long as I could and escaped to the safety of the bunkhouse again as a limbo dance started up in the tent.

I was sure they were all wondering what the heck I was doing here. I had not lifted one finger to help out at the camp and I had not really spoken to anyone. Some of the senior counsellors had made a few attempts to talk but I had been very vague and not much company because I could have simply bawled.

As I lay in the bed in the dark I sobbed uncontrollably and hoped I would be asleep before any of them came back. It was only about 9pm so there was not much chance that I would be "caught". Again I was exhausted and went into a fitful sleep.

In the morning I told myself if things were no better I would have to go home. I felt bad because I would have to leave two of the counsellors without a ride but I had to get out of here. I weighed some options including staying in a hotel in Sydney, away from the camp. I had never been like this before – I felt like I was letting everyone down, including myself. The worst part was, no-body knew – at least I didn't think they knew.

The bell was ringing again. Today had to be better; I made myself believe that. I showered and went off to breakfast again. The morning was starting out OK. I wasn't overwhelmed with sadness. It was still lingering under the surface, but I believed I could control it. If I didn't snap out of it, people would think I couldn't be around the burn-injured children, and that was so far from the truth. They were all beautiful, so carefree and happy at camp.

The kids were supposed to start making cardboard boats for the boat races that would be held in a couple of days, and would keep them busy for a few hours. I sat for a while with the kitchen staff as they enjoyed their breakfast. I engaged in a little small talk, however I was still not acting like myself. I went back up to the bunkhouse with the intention of doing some of the laundry and cleaning the bathrooms. The tasks kept my mind occupied and I was starting to feel like I could survive at camp at least for the day.

Everyone was so nice, smiling and laughing. Most of the staff and counsellors were firefighters or paramedics or worked in the medical field, some were teachers and many were long-time vol-unteers at the camp. You could tell by how it was organized that it was run like a well-oiled machine. Why could I not be happy? There was nothing here to make me sad!

By lunchtime I was feeling a bit closer to normal and decided to try and enjoy the dining hall. I cleaned up and went down for lunch when the bell began to ring. I could almost see the excitement in the air, the kids were chattering about their boats and about the fact that the next day was Christmas. Wow, these people had it all planned out. The kids were talking about how amazing Christmas was the year before and that they couldn't wait. I listened to them and talked a bit to the counsellors on either side of me and felt that I was starting to improve. When lunch was over and the kids got busy again with other activities I helped out with the dishes.

I walked out into the field where the kids were playing volleyball and making boats and I started to feel the surge of sadness well up inside me again. I decided to try and walk it off. Out the road I went again and this time I was able to contain the sadness for a little longer. I swallowed often to keep it down and concentrated on the ripples on the water and the boats in the distance. However it was not enough. I was overwhelmed again and the tears streamed down my face as I cried silently while walking along the dirt road. A light rain began to fall and I didn't have to turn my head as vehicles passed because they wouldn't be able to tell that it was tears. I could not last another few days like this and I was doing nobody any good whatsoever, including myself.

If I couldn't control this I would have to go home. There was no other option. I made up my mind that I would go home in the morning. I was sure somebody would take me to the ferry and I would drive across the Island by myself; maybe that time alone would banish whatever was happening to me. I felt better as I got back because I knew what I had to do. I would either tell the truth or make up some excuse and leave the next day. I could wait until morning, leaving no time for explaining what was happening if I chose.

That evening as we held hands in the tent in the semi-darkness the children and adults started to sing the camp song and it was nearly my undoing. I managed to hang on long enough to get through the song and get out of the tent. That was it, I was going home out of here and away from whatever this despair and sadness was that had overtaken my mind and soul. Maybe I was sick or had something wrong with me and maybe it had nothing to do with camp.

I walked up the path with the light from the open bunkhouse door like a beacon calling me to refuge. I couldn't hold it in any more, the tears fell; I kept my back straight in case anyone in the tent could see me silhouetted in the light and I wept silently as I climbed the steps.

I was so relieved to make it that I didn't notice at first that I wasn't alone. One of the counsellors, a nurse, was in the room working diligently on her laptop. I forgot that the daily newsletter was underway and that she would be working on it this late. Luckily she didn't look up.

I turned my head towards the bunk and grabbed my pajamas, quickly getting into them. I unzipped the sleeping bag and I heard her ask, "Are you going to bed?"

"Yes," I said, "I am tired."

I got settled in the bunk bed and turned in to the wall again without ever turning to face her. I was swallowing hard now so that I wouldn't make any noise. I didn't want her to hear me cry. I could hear her fingers making tapping noises on the keyboard. The pillow beneath my head grew soaked with tears.

These people were so nice and were putting so much work into the camp that I felt horrible not being part of it. I could offer so much help and have so much fun if I would just stop this darn crying. I heard her say she would be finished soon if she was bothering me and, when I could get my breath, I muttered it was fine.

As I concentrated on the keystrokes and thought about the words she was putting to paper I realized that I would never be part of that newsletter because I had never been part of the camp.

Not because of anyone else but because of me. This could be a turning point for me at camp if I would just tell her I was sad. Just say it out loud. I had the opportunity now if I would only reach out and grab it.

I didn't want to, I had never done that before, never reached out for help, never needed help and I thought that made me strong.

I wasn't going to do it now either, I'd go home tomorrow and nobody would ever know. They would think I was a snob, or that I wasn't cut out for camp, or whatever they liked.

A battle was going on in my mind as the tears slowly dried – I had nothing left. Should I say something, should I not? By not saying anything I would continue to spiral out of control in this misery that was new to me. I could say something and take my chances.

The sounds of the keyboard ceased and I heard the sounds of shoes scraping on the floor as the counsellor got to her feet.

Now is my chance – no I won't say anything. Now is my chance – no I won't say anything.

I heard her put the laptop away and as she came towards my bunk to leave the room I turned over and looked up at her. "I am having a really hard time here, I need help." There it was out before I could stop it.

She looked at me and knew that I was crying. As a nurse her Florence Nightingale instinct must have kicked in because she immediately came to me and sat on the bunk near my head and said, "Oh honey, what is wrong!"

"I wish I knew, I don't know what is wrong with me, I have been crying since Monday!"

She took my hand and held on to it as more tears came from somewhere deep within me and I couldn't stop it. Tears streamed down my face and she just sat there holding my hand. After a few minutes I got myself under control and she started asking me questions and just talking about random stuff to keep me calm. I told her about the fire and about being burned at fifteen and how I never cry about it, until now.

She asked if I would mind if she told the other women in the room. I shook my head and said I was OK with that. She said they would help me get through the rest of the week and said she wished I had told them sooner. There was no need to be suffering. I said it was my stubborn "I can do it by myself" streak. We talked some more before she left and I fell into a solid sleep, at peace for the first time since Sunday night.

The next morning I was up with the bell and so were the others. They all started talking to me about ordinary things including what we would be doing that day and what they needed help with, and for the first time since I got there, I let myself be included in the conversation. I discovered there was no need for me to isolate myself. If I was having trouble one of them would come with me to wherever I needed to go and would keep me company. For some reason I knew I would be fine today.

After my shower, I pulled on the tank top that came with my bathing suit and I pulled off the tags. I went outdoors and stood on the step in the sunshine. The birds were chirping out a good morning and the campers were slowly starting to come out and about from the small cabins they had inhabited. The sun shone on my arms for the first time in over twenty-seven years. I looked around to see if anyone would look at me funny, but in this group of campers that would never happen. I slowly made my way down the path towards the dining hall and I met the camp leader coming up the path.

He wished me a good morning, stopped and backed up to where I stood. He looked at me and said, "I didn't realize that you had burns." I nodded, surprisingly not feeling sad or out of place. He asked me to come up to the office with him. I followed him and he invited me to sit. He turned and asked me how I had gotten burned and I told him. I wasn't sad today which was a relief.

I told him that I had been having a very hard time for the last couple of days, sad and crying. He said with a smile that he had been wondering a few times where I had gone. He asked if I was OK and I said I was. He told me that he was very sorry to hear about my family and that he wanted me to have a great camp experience so today would be my "first day." Then he walked me down to the dining hall for breakfast.

As I walked through the door into the crowded space I was expecting everyone would stop and the place would go silent when they realized I had burns. Nothing happened, the world didn't stop, and life went on.

One of the younger kids had just cleaned his plate and was about to leave the hall. As he was passing he said, "Oh, you're burned too, cool!" and that summed it up. I went and got my breakfast plate and nobody looked sideways at me or glanced under their eyes. They smiled and served me. The girls from the bunkhouse asked me to sit with them and I could feel a change come over me from the inside out.

It is very hard to describe the feeling. It was like a weight that I had been carrying for so long, that I didn't know I had, was lifting from inside me and I was seeing the world with new eyes – eyes that weren't watching for somebody to look at me wondering what had happened, or if I had something that was catching. There was a world of love here and I felt part of it that day.

One of the teenaged girls came to stand next to me just after lunch and she put her head on my shoulder. She lightly rubbed her hand up and down one of my arms and she started to cry. She sobbed uncontrollably almost like I had been doing for the last couple of days. I stood there and placed my other hand on her face which rested on my shoulder and let her cry.

I said, "I know exactly how you feel," because I did.

She had had her arm burned as well when she was younger and for some reason saw herself reflected in my burns. She wiped her tears and asked me about my burns, what had happened, and I told her. She told me how she had gotten her burns too. We both stood there as other counsellors came around and we all had a group hug and laughed and cried at the same time.

When I called home that evening Thomas asked me what had changed; he could tell by my voice that I was feeling better. I told him and he was glad for me and hoped I enjoyed the rest of camp. I told him I was confident that I would. That night I got through the camp song without crying and I was able to sing along – out loud. I stayed in the tent all night until the DJ shut down; I danced and did the limbo and felt like I belonged. I laughed and had fun and totally enjoyed the night.

For the rest of the camp experience I joined in with the kids as they played, I helped out as much as I could and I felt so comfortable and included. It was amazing. We had a day boating on the river, the Easter Bunny came, Santa visited, on Carnival day local businesses came with games and prizes for the kids and nearby residents and local firefighters came as well, filling the tent. I wore my camp T-shirt with no long sleeves under it – a milestone for me. The most fabulous fireworks I had ever seen finished off the night. And every evening began with the camp song.

Everyone at camp commented that they noticed the change in me and how much the kids enjoyed my company. They were all happy for me and so glad that I stayed. I was too, I felt uplifted and rejuvenated. I was transformed. I felt free. I felt strong.

Scars tell us more about the future than the past, about how
we can live strong despite any pain we've been through.
~ Terri Guillemets

As we said our goodbyes at the end of the week, I made a commitment to myself that my life was going to change, at least on the inside. I got home Sunday around noon and Thomas and the girls were excited to see me and I was happy to be home. I had a newfound internal strength that I wanted to share with them. I told them all about camp and the activities, which they were very excited to hear. I had on my camp T-shirt without the usual something long-sleeved underneath. I told the girls I wanted to go to the mall with it on. They hugged me and said they were so proud and Thomas said we weren't going without him.

The Village Mall was usually less populated than the Avalon Mall, so I said although I had big intentions I didn't want to overdo it and we all laughed. So the Village Mall it was.

As we got nearer I started to get nervous. Would people stare at me, would it be uncomfortable? Whatever, there had to be a first time and I wasn't backing out now. The euphoria from the camp remained and I wanted to act while it was still with me.

When I stepped out of the car I could feel the wind on my bare arms. It was a strange feeling and I was conscious of the scarred skin. My gaze flicked around to see if anyone was looking and the girls said in unison, "Come on Mom, you can do it."

Wow, the simple act of walking into a mall with a T-shirt on. How could this little thing be such a big deal? But it was! For more than half my life I had covered up to keep away stares and comments. Long sleeves protected me, and made me the same as everyone else. That was about to change.

As we walked in through the main doors I could hear loud music and the crowds were unbelievable. As it turned out, the Village Mall's management had decided to have a concert in center court to draw more people. Instead of being relatively quiet it was like Christmas in here; the place was blocked with people.

I was thinking of leaving, and then I said to myself, *This is a sign*, and I looked up towards the heavens and muttered, "Thanks a lot!" as I went forward into the crowd. Holding my back straight, I walked into the middle of the swarm of people and braced myself for the stares. I thought the music was going to stop and everyone was going to turn and point to me and ask what was wrong with me. However nobody took any notice of me. The concert continued. I wasn't that important!

The girls stood around me like sentries, daring anyone to say something to their mother. Thomas stood by my side and whispered that he was proud of me. I felt good. This was a new day and a new age for me. I had been reborn.

Photo by Ned Pratt

When I thought about it later I realized that I had never really cried about my whole experience. I think that seeing the kids at camp, being so happy and carefree as they played in tanks and shorts and wore their scars so proudly as if there was no reason in the world not to, had a great impact on me. I knew it should have been me too; there was no reason for it not to be.

I had never grieved for my family, or cried for the young girl who had lost her childhood and had been catapulted into a world of tremendous physical and mental torment and change – forced to grow up. I had tried to be so strong for everyone else that I had not given myself time to heal. When my world had moved forward after the fire I had been months behind everyone else. People who had started to deal with their hurt had been in a different place than I was when I got home from the hospital. Nobody talked about the fire, about Francis, Richard, Sharon, Harold or Barry being gone and I didn't want to set them back. The house was gone, I was put into another school, another routine, the hospital, the surgeries, college, and I became the center of attention when I was used to being only one of ten. There was safety and anonymity in being one of ten.

I had to be strong because I thought everyone was looking to me to be strong. I had to be strong because the physical toll the burns had taken on my body could have easily taken my life if I wasn't. I had to be strong for my mother and father because they had lost so much I did not want them to worry about me too. I felt responsible for the wellbeing of my parents, I had to be strong and not complain so that their lives could be just a tiny bit easier. I felt this was my small sacrifice for having them in my life, and I never talked about that with anybody. It was something I felt I needed to do.

Later, I had to be strong for my own family, my girls when we had so little and they deserved so much, and later again when I went back to school to try and make a better life for the family. I had to be strong to stay alive and I never learned how "not to be strong."

That dam had burst when I went to burn camp and saw so many like myself who didn't feel like they had to be strong, but who looked normal and happy like I should allow myself to be. I was alive, I had survived and I could be happy.

In order to get through the anguish, I had to go through the anguish – a place I had never dared go through before nor had I really known existed. When I thought of those first three days at camp I realized that I had probably grieved for the first time since my loss. It was my loss, not just my parents' loss, my family's loss, my community's loss – it was mine too.

I also realized that I had to forgive myself for living – for being alive. Once I was able to forgive myself I was able to be truly alive. I survived a tragedy: it was OK to survive.

This was my epiphany!

Since camp a lot of things have changed for me. Things still get hard sometimes but they don't define me – they are circumstances, not a way of life. I know that now.

Some people say that it must have been difficult to write this and it was, but I am glad I shared the story. I hope that my life's journey to this point will help others who may feel they are victims realize that it is possible to come out the other side. You have to go through it in order to get through it, no matter what that "it" might be. Being stuck somewhere in the middle is existence and not living, there is a difference.

I think of Francis, Richard, Sharon, Harold and Barry often especially on birthdays and in June. They mattered to a lot of people.

This is not the end but it is beyond the beginning, beyond several beginnings. I am stronger now than I have ever been. I am a survivor by choice on the inside and out.

Epilogue

It was the strangest place, like we were all in a black room and I couldn't tell if the walls were close or far away or if there were walls at all. It was just black.

Inside this black space all my brothers and sisters were standing side by side in a row facing me. Although I was the one looking at the lineup, I was also standing in the lineup. My parents were not there.

The line was formed in order of birth, all of us looking towards where I stood, and we were all wearing our normal clothes. It was unusual that I was looking on, especially since I could see myself in the line between Larry and Sharon; however it felt like I should be in both places.

Surrounding the entire gathering, including me from where I was looking on, was what appeared to be a ring of fire. Although I didn't turn my head I could tell it was a perfect circle. The glow seemed to emanate from behind me and in my peripheral vision, as I looked at my family in the lineup, I could see the ring of fire go right around.

As I moved towards the lineup it felt very strange as if I were floating. I knew I wasn't walking; however, I was moving.

It was almost like an army sergeant inspecting the troops. I started with Mary, who was standing there, not seeing who or what I was. In my thoughts, without speaking aloud, a voice said, *You will be safe, you won't be there.*

I moved to Eddy. *You will be safe and you will be happy.*

Then I got to Francis. *You will die!* Francis was also standing unseeing so there was no reaction from him.

I came to Neil. *You will be safe and you will be happy.*

Next there was Richard. *You will die!*

I moved to Larry. *You will be safe because you need to have a happy life.*

Then I stood in front of myself. *You will die!* This did not affect me as I stood there again unseeing and it did not affect me as the person making the declaration.

I moved on to Sharon. *You will die!* Instead of moving to Harold, I turned back and stood in front of myself again. *You will live but you will not be safe. You will be the strength your parents need to move forward.*

I moved past Sharon, to Harold and Barry. *You will die!* The ring of fire glowed closer and closer and I could see the flickering of the glow of the fire on the sides of their faces.

I then moved back to where I had started and the circle of fire moved out as I moved back. The room remained so black that I couldn't tell how big it was and my family were each standing still in the line staring straight ahead.

Things got hazy and I could hear my mother shouting out from the bottom of the stairs. "Toast and tea everyone! It's time to get up! After today you will have your summer holidays."

I shook Sharon as I bolted out of bed. Today was the last day of school. We would get our report cards and say goodbye to our classmates and friends until next year – which was really September to a Grade 10 student.

We usually all ran to the top of the stairs to see who would get down first and myself and Sharon had the advantage because we were closest. As chaos ensued at the table and the smell of homemade bread toast filled the air I thought no more of my dream.

Today was June 18th, 1980; the last day of school! One more year and I would have to make my way in the world and make decisions over what I wanted to be when I grew up. One more year of school and I would have reached "grown up" status.

As five of us gathered our things to race to the bus, filled with the excitement and prospects of summer, we were innocent to the fact that this would be the last day of some of our lives, and the last day that things would be normal for the Linehans, or anyone else in North Harbour, St. Mary's Bay.

Photo by Ned Pratt

Ida Linehan Young grew up in North Harbour, St. Mary's Bay, Newfoundland and lived in St. Bride's, Placentia Bay for an number of years before making her home in Conception Bay South with her husband and three daughters. She currently works with the Federal Government and her passions include community volunteer work and do-it-yourself home renovations.

Linehan Family Album

*"Wherever a beautiful soul has been
there is a trail of beautiful memories."*

~ Nishan Panwar

Francis

Richard

Sharon

Harold

Barry

Mary

Eddy

Neil

Larry

Ida

Ida

Nanny and Grandfather Power, Frank and Ida.

Dad on his motorcycle returning from work.

Sharon, Mom and Ida.

Mr. Jer, Jerimiah Bonia.

Nanny and Grandfather with Francis.

Sharon, Ida, Barry and Harold.

Richard, Neil, Ida and Barry.

Mary, Francis, Sharon, Harold and Ida.

Neil and Richard.

Neil, Francis, Richard, Sharon, Ida, Harold and Barry.

Harold and Barry.

Eddy, Francis, Neil and Richard.

Ida, Sharon, Harold and Barry.

Francis

Sharon, Ida and Harold.

Francis, Harold and Barry.

Francis looking up the stairs.

Francis in his cast.

Mary

THE TOP

EDWARD LINEHAN

Ida with her parents, Eddy and Catherine,
at her high school graduation in 1981.

Dad